Working Together for Local Integration of Migrants and Refugees in Paris

This document, as well as any data and any map included herein, are without prejudice to the status of or sovereignty over any territory, to the delimitation of international frontiers and boundaries and to the name of any territory, city or area.

Please cite this publication as:
OECD (2018), *Working Together for Local Integration of Migrants and Refugees in Paris*, OECD Publishing, Paris.
https://doi.org/10.1787/9789264305861-en

ISBN 978-92-64-30585-4 (print)
ISBN 978-92-64-30586-1 (PDF)

The statistical data for Israel are supplied by and under the responsibility of the relevant Israeli authorities. The use of such data by the OECD is without prejudice to the status of the Golan Heights, East Jerusalem and Israeli settlements in the West Bank under the terms of international law.

Photo credits: Cover © Marianne Colombani

Corrigenda to OECD publications may be found on line at: *www.oecd.org/about/publishing/corrigenda.htm*.

© OECD 2018

You can copy, download or print OECD content for your own use, and you can include excerpts from OECD publications, databases and multimedia products in your own documents, presentations, blogs, websites and teaching materials, provided that suitable acknowledgment of the source and copyright owner(s) is given. All requests for public or commercial use and translation rights should be submitted to *rights@oecd.org*. Requests for permission to photocopy portions of this material for public or commercial use shall be addressed directly to the Copyright Clearance Center (CCC) at *info@copyright.com* or the Centre francais d'exploitation du droit de copie (CFC) at *contact@cfcopies.com*.

Foreword

When it comes to migrant integration, the local level matters. Where migrants go and how they integrate into their new communities depends on the specific characteristics of cities and regions. Even though migration policies are the responsibility of the national government, the concentration of migrants in cities, and particularly in metropolitan areas, has an impact on the local demand for work, housing, goods and services that local authorities have to manage. Local authorities play a vital role in this integration. Cities can learn from each other and help provide local, regional, national and international policy makers and practitioners with better evidence for integration policy design.

This case study *Working Together for Local Integration of Migrants and Refugees in Paris* provides insight into the city's migrant integration trends and current situation. In order to do so, it applies the OECD *Checklist for public action to migrant integration at the local level* that is articulated around 4 blocks and 12 objectives. The four blocks cover: 1) institutional and financial settings; 2) time and proximity as keys for migrants and host communities to live together; 3) enabling conditions for policy formulation and implementation; and 4) sectoral policies related to integration: access to the labour market, housing, social welfare and health, and education.

This case study is part of a broader OECD-European Union project "A territorial approach to migrant integration: The role of local authorities" which addresses a critical gap in knowledge on migration issues by analysing the multi-level governance of local integration. The project takes stock of such multi-level governance frameworks and policies for migrant and refugee integration at the local level in nine large European cities: Amsterdam, Athens, Barcelona, Berlin, Glasgow, Gothenburg, Paris, Rome and Vienna and, thanks to the support of the German Ministry for Economic Affairs and Energy, a small city in Germany (Altena). It also builds on information collected from these and 61 other European cities, through an ad-hoc survey and a newly created and publicly available statistical database on migrant outcomes at regional level. The project looks at updates to the governance mechanisms that cities adopted in the wake of the influx of asylum seekers and refugees that concerned EU countries since 2015. Conversely, it also investigates opportunities to extend some of the services recently established for newcomers to long-standing migrant groups.

This and the other nine city case studies, along with the synthesis report *Working Together for Local Integration of Migrants and Refugees,* are outputs of this OECD European Union initiative contributing to the programme of work of the OECD Regional Development Policy Committee (RDPC) implemented by the Centre for Entrepreneurship, SMEs, Regions and Cities (CFE). They also contribute to the OECD Horizontal Project on "Ensuring the effective integration of vulnerable migrant groups" by focusing on improving the integration capacities of the local governments.

Acknowledgements

This publication *Working Together for Local Integration of Migrants and Refugees in Paris* was produced by the Centre for Entrepreneurship, SMEs, Regions and Cities (CFE) led by Lamia Kamal-Chaoui, Director. It is part of a wider project "A territorial approach to migrant integration: The role of local authorities" and an output of an OECD European Union initiative contributing to the programme of work of the OECD's Regional Development Policy Committee (RDPC).

Co-ordination of the wider project and this case study was led by Claire Charbit, Head of the Territorial Dialogue and Migration Unit in the Regional Development and Tourism Division managed by Alain Dupeyras, in CFE. This case study was drafted by Anna Piccinni, Maria Trullén Malaret and Gaetan Muller (OECD). It benefitted from substantial inputs made by Charlotte Demuijnck, Paola Proietti, Vivianne Spitzhofer, Lisanne Raderschall and Marcos Diaz-Ramirez (OECD). This case study also benefitted from the comments of other OECD directorates and in particular from Cécile Thoreau, International Migration Division of the Directorate for Employment, Labour and Social Affairs (ELS).

This case study has been developed thanks to the close collaboration of the municipality of Paris that provided the information and organised meetings for the OECD field work, as well as the support of the national government officials who provided information. The Secretariat would like to express its gratitude to all participants to the interviews (see Annex 1). In particular, the OECD thanks Dominique Versini, Deputy Mayor of Paris for Solidarity, the Fight Against Exclusion, Refugee Reception and Child Protection, for her ongoing support throughout the process of the case study as well as to Anne-Charlotte Leluc and Charlotte Schneider, members of her team.

The Secretariat is especially thankful for the financial contribution and the collaboration throughout the implementation of the project to the European Union Directorate-General for Regional and Urban Policy. In particular, the Secretariat would like to thank Andor Urmos for their guidance as well as for their substantive inputs to the revision of the case study.

Table of contents

Tables

Figures

Boxes

Abbreviations and acronyms

ADA	Allocation pour demandeur d'asile
AME	Aide médicale d'État
APUR	Atelier parisien d'urbanisme
ARS	Agence régionale de santé
CADA	Centre d'accueil pour demandeurs d'asile
CAF	Caisse d'allocations familiales
CAO	Centre d'accueil et orientation
CASNAV	Centres académiques pour la scolarisation des enfants allophones nouvellement Arrivés et des enfants issus de familles itinérantes et voyageurs
CASVP	Centre d'action sociale de la ville de Paris CCAS : Centre communal d'action sociale
CGET	Commissariat général à l'égalité des territoires
CHU	Centre d'hébergement d'urgence
CHUM	Centre d'hébergement d'urgence pour migrants
CII	Comité interministériel à l'intégration
CIR	Contrat d'intégration républicaine
CMS	Centres municipaux de santé
COPIL	Comité de pilotage
CPA	Centre de premier accueil
CPEF	Centre de planification d'éducation familiale
CPH	Centre provisoire d'hébergement
CROUS	Centre régional des œuvres universitaires et scolaires
DAC	Direction des affaires culturelles
DAE	Direction de l'attractivité et de l'emploi
DAEEN	Direction de l'accueil, de l'accompagnement des étrangers et de la nationalité (Ministère de l'Intérieur)
DASCO	Direction des affaires scolaires
DASES	Direction de l'action Sociale, de l'enfance et de la santé
DDCS	Direction départementale de la cohésion sociale de Paris
DDCT	Direction de la démocratie, des citoyennes et des territoires
DFPE	Direction de la famille et de la petite enfance

DGEF	Direction générale des étrangers en France (Ministère de l'Intérieur)
DGESCO	Direction générale de l'enseignement scolaire (Ministère de l'éducation nationale)
DIHAL	Délégation interministérielle à l'hébergement et à l'accès au logement
DLH	Direction du logement et de l'habitat
DPVI	Délégation politique de la ville et intégration
DU	Direction de l'urbanisme
ENIC-NARIC	Centre français d'information sur la reconnaissance académique et professionnelle des diplômes
EPCI	Établissement public de coopération intercommunale
FMI	Fonds asile, migration et intégration
FSL	Fonds de solidarité pour le logement
FTDA	France terre d'asile
FTM	Foyer travailleurs migrants
GUDA	Guichet unique d'accueil des demandeurs d'asile
HCR	Haut-Commissariat pour les réfugiés des Nations Unies
HOPE	Programme hébergement, orientation et parcours vers l'emploi
INSEE	Institut national de la statistique et des études économiques
MGP	Métropole du Grand Paris
OCDE	Organisation de coopération et de développement économique
OFII	Office français de l'immigration et de l'intégration
OFPRA	Office français de protection des réfugiés et apatrides
OPRE	Ouvrir l'école aux parents pour la réussite des enfants
PAD	Point d'accès au Droit
PADA	Plateforme d'accueil des demandeurs d'asile
PASS	Permanences d'accès aux soins de santé PUMA : Protection universelle maladie
PIMMS	Points d'information et de médiation multiservices
RAD	Relais d'accès au droit
RSA	Revenu de solidarité active
SIAO	Services intégrés d'accueil et d'orientation
SRADAR	Schéma régional de l'accueil des demandeurs d'asile et à l'intégration des réfugiés
UNESCO	Organisation des Nations Unis pour l'éducation, la science et la culture
UPE2A	Unités pédagogiques pour élèves allophones arrivants

Executive summary

The region Ile-de-France, represents close to a fifth (18.1%) of the French population. Of the region's 12 million inhabitants, around 2.2 million live in Paris. The Ile-de-France region accounts for almost 40% of all foreigners present in mainland France. Within Paris, around 20% of the population is foreign born, among which more than a third have acquired French nationality. Migrants, asylum seekers and refugees have arrived in successive waves and tend to cluster in distinct neighbourhoods of the city, often by nationality. The largest migrant groups are from Algeria, China, Portugal, Morocco and Italy. Almost 80% of total foreign-born population in Ile-de-France settled more than ten years ago.

Since 2015, and like many urban centres in Europe, Paris experienced an increase in humanitarian migrants. Out of the almost 64 000 asylum requests made in 2016 in France, around 24 000 were made in the region of Ile-de-France, over 40% of which were in Paris (approximately 10 000). The increase of arrivals has put pressure on public services and called for both emergency and long-term integration responses.

Recent trends have to be understood within the City of Paris (hereafter the City) approach to integration issues. France traditionally has sought to integrate migrants through uniform policies, meaning through access for all groups to universal services. Since 2015, there has been an increased awareness at all levels of government that migrants and refugees need additional and targeted support above and beyond equitable access to universal services for social and job market integration. The creation in 2018 of the Interministerial Integration Committee and the Inter-ministerial Delegate for Refugee Reception and Integration attests to this shift in integration policy. Integration has returned among the priorities of the French administration, with an awareness that the territorial dimension is crucial. The challenge is to combine the means and measures that will be at the disposal of regional *préfets* (representatives of the national government in the region) with the actions that cities already deploy.

At the local level, while the principle of universal access to services is maintained, the City has put in place a variety of actions to facilitate and accompany migrants in accessing those services. In addition, the City deploys actions targeting broader objectives of social cohesion, such as trying to foster the inclusion of migrant communities and fighting isolation, including by increasing the likelihood for migrants to interact with the native born.

Whereas the national government holds key competences in migration and asylum policy, the City is responsible for key sectors (i.e. social and welfare services, etc.) relevant to integration. It does so both as a "*départment*" (second tier of subnational government) and a municipality. Within this multi-level governance framework, the City acts in support of migrants, closely collaborating with numerous Paris-based non-governmental organisations (NGOs) active throughout different stages of a migrant's reception and integration journey.

The municipality of Paris uses different policy tools to attract and integrate migrants who choose the city as their destination. This report investigates in particular three of them. First, the report describes some of the generic services that each municipal department is financing which have an impact on migrant access to public services. It also considers the co-ordination system that ensures their coherence. The City monitors these services through an action plan for integration and allocates a specific budget that has been multiplied by four since 2005. Concretely, this action plan does not finance a parallel migrant-specific system. Rather, it ensures a plurality of entry points for migrants in the city to access their social and legal rights over time and navigate bureaucratic procedures.

Second, the report considers the City Policy (*Politique de la ville*), a national-urban policy which aims at reducing intra-urban inequalities by strengthening the quality of public services offered in the most deprived neighbourhoods. The City of Paris comanages and co-finances this policy with the national government. This policy significantly affects the integration of migrants as they are over-represented in such areas.

Third, the report explores the city's new action plan "Mobilisation of the Paris Community for Refugee Reception". Paris has responded to the 2015 increase of humanitarian migrant arrivals with this plan to improve reception and integration of asylum seekers and refugees. It falls under the responsibility of the Deputy Mayor in charge of "Solidarity, the Fight Against Exclusion, Child Protection and Refugee Reception".

Key findings

Some remaining challenges

Segregation and inclusion

Socio-economic disparities and spatial segregation are stark in Paris and represent a key barrier to integration. The unemployment rate in the Ile-de France region is nearly double for foreign-born persons as compared to those who are native born. The metropolitan area of Greater Paris (around 7 million inhabitants) has the highest income inequalities among French metropolitan areas. Within the metropolitan area of Paris, it is in the city of Paris where those inequalities are widest. The Northeast neighbourhoods concentrate high unemployment rates and social housing, whereas centre and western districts and most of the southern districts are more affluent. Migrant residents are highly concentrated in those areas facing more socioeconomic difficulties. In the most economically deprived neighbourhoods (i.e. targeted by the City Policy), 30% of residents are foreign born, 10 percentage points more than the city's average.

The City has implemented several initiatives to address segregation and inclusion. To reduce the feeling of separation and decrease prejudice across neighbourhoods, the City of Paris engaged in a communications campaign. The most deprived neighbourhoods were renamed as "the must-go zones" in response to a U.S. television reference that these neighbourhoods were "no-go zones". The City also implements short-term initiatives to spur day-to-day interactions across communities by creating attractive public spaces for all, particularly in those areas. Nevertheless, more long-term inclusion will be the result of smart spatial and housing planning that creates affordable and attractive solutions where different groups can live together. The City of Paris, together with the City of Gothenburg are amongst the most innovative cities in the sample of this study in terms of designing housing solutions that factor-in the well-being of all groups and that foster urban cohesion.

Limited capacity of emergency accommodation facilities and access to adequate housing

Migrants account for two thirds of the total homeless population in Paris. The peak of arrivals since 2015 has increased the number of migrants living in spontaneous camps throughout the city and in particular in the northeast area. As of March 2018, around 1 900 migrants were estimated to be living in such conditions in Paris. Some of them were asylum seekers who cannot access the French asylum system because they have been registered in other EU countries under Dublin regulations, and others could not be sheltered in the national reception system because of its limited accommodation capacities.

What is already done and how it could be improved

The need for a holistic and multi-level national approach to the integration of migrants and refugees

The approach to migrant integration at the national level aims at easing access to universal services for all groups rather than creating specific policies targeting migrants. A significant exception to this uniform approach is the Contract of Republican Integration (*Contrat d'intégration républicaine - CIR*) which has existed since 2007. This contract mainly focuses on the provision of language classes and takes place during the first five years of a migrant's residence in the country. The CIR is usually not implemented in coordination with lower levels of government that often set up local initiatives to fill gaps in the provision of language classes.

However, French authorities are currently reforming the integration system through two main processes. First, in 2018 a Parliamentary report entitled "For an Ambitious Integration Policy of Foreigners arriving in France" calls for a national integration policy. The proposal highlights the current fragmentation of actors participating in the integration of migrants and calls for strong vertical and horizontal coordination. The proposed integration policy foresees to strengthen the CIR by increasing the supply of language learning courses along with simplifying migrants' access to employment, education, health, housing and social welfare services. Second, since 2018 an Inter-ministerial Delegate for Refugee Integration has been embedded within the Ministry of Interior with the mandate to implement the National Strategy for Refugee Integration (2018-2020). The strategy envisages not only a cross-sectoral committee at national level but also local steering committees that will involve *préfets* and local authorities.

Coordination and funding mechanism with non-governmental organisations

Several Paris-based Non-Governmental Organisations (NGOs) provide support in integration-related domains, and many new NGOs emerged since 2015 to respond to refugee arrivals. Since 2015, Paris has tested new coordination modalities with NGOs in managing the reception of asylum seekers and refugees. First, since 2015 the action plan "Mobilisation of the Paris Community for Refugee Reception" is collectively updated and monitored through a platform that brings together, twice a year, the municipality and partner stakeholders involved in the domain. Second, the two first-reception Humanitarian Centres for Asylum Seekers (CPA) set up in 2016 were managed through a multi-stakeholder co-ordination mechanism with NGOs as well as national and local authorities.

Nevertheless, it seems that coordination mechanisms among NGOs and between them and the municipality could be strengthened with regards to long-term integration measures. For instance, sectoral co-ordination platforms for language courses could strengthen the co-operation among NGOs and improve the effectiveness of the classes offered to migrants. The city of Barcelona has implemented such a platform. In terms of funding, grants for migrant integration-related projects tend to be allocated to local NGOs in small amounts and on a short-term basis - often annually. More long-term funding for integration and an effort for streamlining the calls for projects issued from different levels of government and different city departments would allow NGOs to be more sustainable and effective.

Coordination and implementation of a local approach to migrant integration

The municipality sets aside dedicated resources and has an active approach to migrant integration, which places Paris amongst the European cities analysed in this study with the most structured tools to tackle integration. However, more could be done in terms of seeking policy coherence to avoid horizontal fragmentation of policy-making and service delivery. Despite the high number of municipal directorates and policies (i.e. City Policy, Pact to address Exclusion, Pact for Labour Market Inclusion) which have a direct impact on integration, there is no working group to align the objectives and measure of the results that collectively the city is achieving in the long-term in this area.

There are opportunities to better capitalise on the City's efforts through evidence-based decision-making. For instance, by sharing across directorates the experiences of its different social service departments and the information collected through the integration budget, the City could collectively identify the gaps. It could then formulate joint strategies and policies around a "road-map approach" which ensures migrants' equal access to services over time. This approach could be mainstreamed in relevant policy portfolios and orient operational services towards the standards they need to meet, such as improving linkages across administrations and transfer of information, among others. Examples of evidence-based decision making that could serve as an example can be found in the case study on the City of Gothenburg.

Good practices that could be replicated

Fostering proximity and connection between recently arrived and native-born residents

The integration process concerns both migrants and native-born communities. Since 2015, the municipality together with civil society organisations has implemented innovative pilot projects to bridge the divides and create proximity between long established communities and newcomers.

First, the City facilitates matching between the offer of and the demand for volunteer work through the web platform *"Je m'engage"* (in English: "I commit") launched in 2015. Second, the city invests in public spaces that can encourage interaction across groups. The municipality supported the creation of spaces where different communities could meet, share their interests and where new talents could emerge, often reviving sites in disadvantaged neighbourhoods. Two noteworthy examples include the cultural centre "104" created in early 2000s, in a neighbourhood characterised by a strong presence of migrants. The "*Les grands voisins*" ("The Big Neighbours") is a project that revived an old hospital area close to the centre of Paris using the space as a shelter for refugees, as well as start-ups, artist workshops, restaurants and bars, attracting Parisians and migrants alike thanks to its innovative use of space.

Ensuring migrant and refugee access to services over time

A priority of Paris in its approach to the integration of migrants is the elimination of obstacles to citizenship and social and legal rights. This is done by offering targeted legal assistance and making sure universal services, in particular social services, are adapted to migrant needs. The objective is to guarantee over time that migrants can access universal services on their own. For instance the city has invested in several mechanisms to facilitate access to residence permits, such as through free legal consultation services, translation of administrative documents, etc. Furthermore, the city has implemented entry points to guide vulnerable residents through universal services such as the multi-service mediation and information points (PIMMS) to ensure that the most vulnerable groups living in disadvantaged neighbourhoods can access their rights or the "Mobile City Council" which visits three sites per week in disadvantaged areas.

Building capacity in the civil service

The municipality is engaged in eliminating administrative and language barriers that migrants might encounter when accessing public services. To do so, trainings are offered to municipal agents in several branches of city government on how to receive users with a foreign background. Since 2004, more than 1 000 municipal officers have been trained to promote equality and combat discrimination. Since 2016, the city has also invested in training for municipal health professionals to address the specific health and social needs of migrants.

Key Data on Migrant Presence and Integration in Paris

Paris is the capital and most populated city in France with 2 220 445 inhabitants. It is located within the region of Île-de-France which gathers 12 246 200 million people. There are 20 municipal districts in Paris called arrondissements which represent the smallest administrative unit.

Figure 1. Paris location in France according to the OECD regional classification

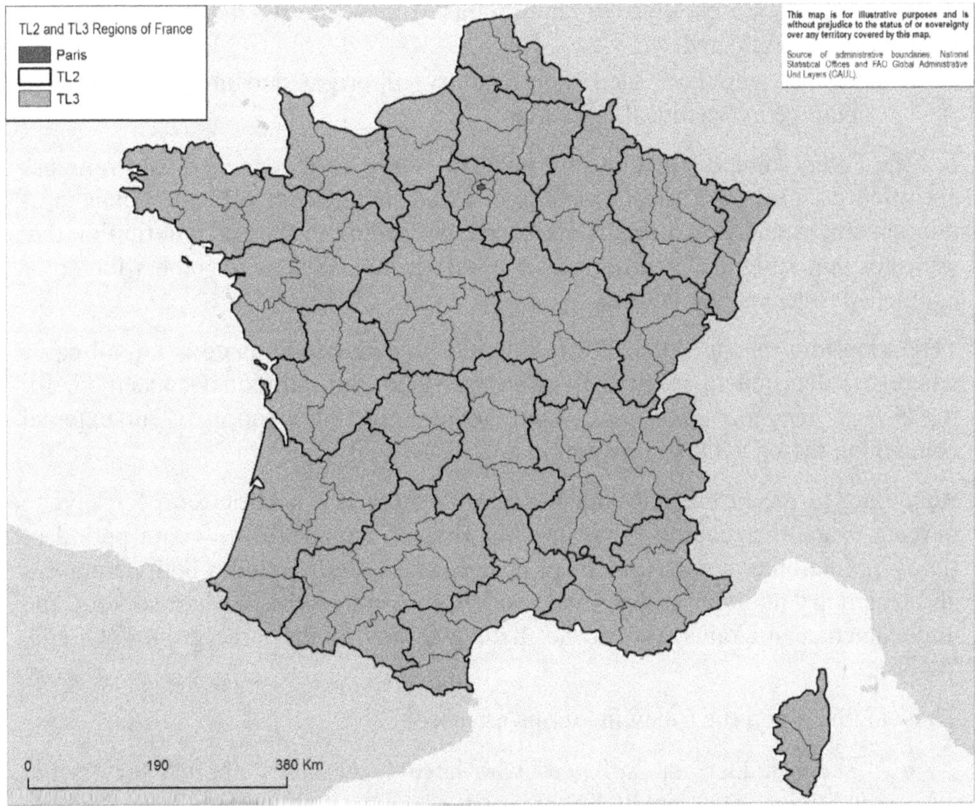

Note: Territorial Level 2 (TL2) consists of the OECD classification of regions within each member country. There are 335 regions classified at this level across 35-member countries. Territorial Level 3 (TL3) consists of the lower level of classification and is composed of 1681 small regions. In most cases, they correspond to administrative regions.
Source: OECD (2018), *OECD Regional Statistics* (database), http://dx.doi.org/10.1787/region-data-en.

Municipality	TL3	TL2	State
Paris	Paris	Île-de-France	France

This section presents key definitions and a selection of indicators about migrant presence and integration in Paris.

Box 1.1. Definition of migrant and refugee

The term "migrant" generally functions as an umbrella term used to describe people that move to another country with the intention of staying for a significant period of time. According to the United Nations (UN), a long-term migrant is "a person who moves to a country other than that of his or her usual residence for a period of at least a year (12 months)" (UNSD, 2017). Yet, not all migrants move for the same reasons, have the same needs or are subject to the same laws.

This report considers migrants a large group that includes:

- Persons who have emigrated to an EU country from another EU country ("EU migrants"),
- Persons who have come to an EU country from a non-EU country ('non-EU born or third-country national'),
- Native-born children of immigrants (often referred to as the "second generation") and
- Persons who have fled their country of origin and are seeking/ have obtained international protection.

For the latter, some distinctions are needed. While asylum seekers and refugees are often counted as a subset of migrants and included in official estimates of migrant stocks and flows, this is not correct according to the UN's definition that indicates that "migrant" does not refer to refugees, displaced, or others forced or compelled to leave their homes:

"The term *migrant* in Article 1.1 (a) should be understood as covering all cases where the decision to migrate is taken freely by the individual concerned, for reasons of *personal convenience* and without the intervention of an external compelling factor" (IOM Constitution Article 1.1 (a)).

According to recent OECD work the term *migrant* is a generic term for anyone moving to another country with the intention of staying for a certain period of time – not, in other words, tourists or business visitors. It includes both permanent and temporary migrants with a valid residence permit or visa, asylum seekers, and undocumented migrants who do not belong to any of the three groups (OECD, 2016b).

Thus, in this report the following terms are used:

- "Status holder" or "refugee" who have successfully applied for asylum and have been granted some sort of protection in their host country, including those who are recognised on the basis of the 1951 Geneva Convention Relating to the Status of Refugees, but also those benefiting from national asylum laws or EU legislation (Directive 2011/95/EU), such as the subsidiary protection status. This corresponds to the category 'humanitarian migrants' meaning recipients of protection – be it refugee status, subsidiarity or temporary protection – as used in recent OECD work (OECD, 2016b).
- "Asylum seeker" for those individuals who have submitted a claim for international protection but are awaiting the final decision.

- "Rejected asylum seeker" for those individuals who have been denied protection status.
- "Undocumented or irregular migrants" for those who do not have a legal permission to stay.

This report systematically distinguishes which group is targeted by policies and services put in place by the city. Where statistics provided by the cities included refugees in the migrant stocks and flows, it will be indicated accordingly.

Statistics in France are based on country of birth and nationality. Three categories are tracked by the French National Institute of Statistics (INSEE) following the recommendations of the High Council for Integration (*Haut conseil à l'intégration*) and here detailed:

1. Migrant population (*immigrés*) according to the definition adopted by the High Council for Integration, are people born outside of France (i.e. foreign-born) and living in France thus referring to country of birth and nationality of birth. The migrant category is permanent and a person continues to be considered migrant even after becoming French by acquisition. This category does not include (1) people born in France of foreign nationality (mostly minors which will acquire the nationality when turning 18), or (2) people born abroad with French nationality at birth (which is a bigger group mostly from the Maghreb). This definition is linked to the French colonial past and France's history of settlement colonies with citizenship right. Recent OECD research makes this category the same as "foreign born" for international comparison purposes (OECD, 2017a). The migrant category is not considered in legislation like in other countries, but has been used for statistical records since 1999. At the local level (*département*), data for the *immigré* category exists uniquely on housing and unemployment.
2. Most of the data at the local level collected in France is based on nationality and refers to the "foreign" population (*population étrangère*) which are people legally living in France but without French nationality (i.e. either having exclusively another nationality or being state-less). Foreign individuals are not always migrants as they might have been born in France from foreign parents. The Foreign category is not life-lasting since foreign persons can become French by acquisition of the nationality. This is the determinant category considered by the French legislation, state services and statistical monitoring.
3. The term "migrant descendent" refers to the population that was born and living in France but with at least one migrant parent (i.e. second generation).

Notes:
INSEE definition of "Immigrant" in France: https://www.insee.fr/fr/metadonnees/definition/c1198.
INSEE definition of "Foreign" in France: https://www.insee.fr/fr/metadonnees/definition/c1328.
Source: Author's elaboration.

Key statistics

- Country subnational government expenditure as a percentage of GDP: 11.4% (2015).
  Subnational spending accounts for 20.1% of public expenditure (2015); The OECD average is 40%.
  Source: OECD, S*subnational government and finance* (database).
- Total population: Paris is the capital of France and its most populated city with a municipal population of 2 220 445 inhabitants. It has a relative small surface of 105 square km and it is composed by 20 districts called arrondissements. The City of Paris corresponds also to the *Département* of Paris (see Figure 2.1).
- Ile-de-France Region (TL2) 12 246 200 inhabitants in 2014.It is home to 18.1% of the French population.
- The Greater Paris – *Métropole du Grand Paris*- is composed by the City of Paris and other 130 municipalities (7 020 010 inhabitants in 2015). It includes the municipalities of the Petite Couronne (close ring) and the three corresponding *départements* - Les Hauts-de-Seine (92), la Seine-Saint-Denis (93) et le Val-de-Marne (94)- and seven municipalities of the Grand Couronne (enlarged ring).

Population trends in Paris

Foreign individuals account for 15% of the population in the city of Paris and immigrants account for 20.4%.

Table 1. Population by nationality and migration background in Paris (2014)

	Number	Share (%)	
French	1 895 346	85.4	
French by birth-Native born population	1694 080	**76.3**	**100% of Paris inhabitants**
French by acquisition	201 266	**9.1**	
Foreign	325 099	**14.6**	
EU	99 404	4.5	
Other European	14 483	0.7	
Maghreb	63 131	2.8	
Other African	52 928	2.4	
Turkey	3 343	0.2	
Other Nationalities	91 811	4.1	
Total	2 220 445	100	

Source: INSEE (2014), *RP 2014.*

The most important countries of origin

Paris is a highly diverse city with more than 150 nationalities represented. Among them, the biggest nationalities in Paris are:

Table 2. Most important countries of origin in Paris (2014)

Origin	Number	Share of foreign population (%)	Share of total population
Algeria	29 853	9	1.3
China	26 892	8.1	1.2
Portugal	26 199	7.9	1.2
Morocco	20 240	6.1	0.9
Italy	17 254	5.2	0.8

Source: Data provided by the municipality to the OECD.

The municipality has indicated that in the past two years, migrants arriving in Paris are mainly coming from Afghanistan, Somalia, Eritrea, Sudan, Democratic Republic of Congo, Mali as well as Chechnya, Georgia and Ukraine.

- **Unaccompanied minors**: 1 500 in 2017 according to the municipality
- **Asylum seekers in the accommodation system in Paris**: 3 907 asylum seekers staying in the Paris accommodation system for asylum seekers (CADA, HUDA, AT-SA) in 2017.

Employment outcomes

The main industrial sectors where migrant work:

Table 3. Breakdown of foreign residents in different activity branches in Paris

Activity Branches	%
Agriculture	0
Craftsmanship, shopkeepers, local business owners	3.2
Executives and intellectual professions	15.3
Intermediary Professions	9.9
Employed	17.4
Workers	9.8
Retired	10
Other residents without professional activity	34.3
Total	100

Source: Provided by the municipality in the OECD Questionnaire.

Table 4. Unemployment rate by nationality, National level, 2015

Nationality	Man	Women
French	9.8	9
Total Foreign	25.9	23.6
Non-EU Foreign	21.2	18.9

Source: INSEE, *Enquête emploi.*

Table 5. Activity status by nationality, Paris, 2014

	Employed	Unemployed	Total
French by birth	825 770	92 980	1 426 566
French by acquisition	107 860	20 162	194 789
European Union (EU 27)	58 763	6 646	100 246
Other European	6 231	1 633	13 041
Maghreb	22 805	8 908	55 997
Other African countries	21 359	6 840	40 987
Turkey	1 254	547	2 987
Other nationalities	44 361	7 971	79 278
Total	1 088 402	145 688	1 903 889

Source: INSEE (2014), *RO2014*.

Table 6. Employment rate, Foreign-born (FB) relative to native-born (NB) in the region of Île-de-France (TL2), 2014-2015

Male		Female		Total	
NB	FB	NB	FB	NB	FB
70	68	66	57	78	62

Source: OECD database on immigrant integration at the regional level.

Table 7. Unemployment Rate, Foreign-born (FB) relative to native-born (NB) in the region of Île-de-France (TL2), 2014-2015

Male		Female		Total	
NB	FB	NB	FB	NB	FB
9	16	7	13	8	14

Source: OECD database on immigrant integration at the regional level.

Table 8. Participation rate, Foreign-born (FB) relative to native-born (NB) in the region of Île-de-France (TL2), 2014-2015

Male		Female		Total	
NB	FB	NB	FB	NB	FB
76	80	71	65	73	72

Source: OECD database on immigrant integration at the regional level.

Education

Table 9. Educational attainment of foreign-born relative to native born in the region of Île-de-France region (TL2), 2014-2015

Native born			Foreign born		
% low-educated	% medium-educated	% highly-educated	% low-educated	% medium-educated	% highly-educated
15	37	47	41	27	32

Note: Educational levels are based on ISCED 1997 ratings, from 0 to 6. A low-education level (0 - 2) reflects a primary education level, a medium-education level (3 - 4) corresponds to a secondary educational attainment and a high-education level (5 - 6) to a tertiary education level.
Source: OECD database on immigrant integration at the regional level.

Income

In Paris, the median disposable income by household is EUR 26 194.7; 16.1% of the overall population is below the poverty rate (Insee, 2015).

Table 10. Average annual income in euros in 2012, In Paris, Île-de-France and France

	Paris	Île—de-France	France
Average annual income (EUR)	31 030	26 411	21 346

Source: INSEE, *DADS.*

Right to vote in Paris

Right to vote or be eligible to national elections is not extended to foreigners in France. European Union nationals living in France can vote and are eligible in European elections (since 1999) and municipal elections (since 2001). This is not the case for non-EU citizens. This is different from some neighbouring European Union countries (e.g. Sweden, Denmark, Belgium or the Netherlands) where non-EU foreigners who have lived continuously in the national territory for a certain number of years can vote for municipal elections; other countries allow foreigners to vote only if there is a reciprocity agreement between the two relevant countries (e.g. Spain and Portugal) when length of stay requirements are met.

Introduction

The increase of international migration in Europe has enhanced public interest about how governments, at all levels, promote the integration of newcomers into host societies. France, and particularly Paris, have historically been migrant destinations and since 2014 the inflows of vulnerable humanitarian migrants increased. The objective of this case study is to provide an analysis of migrant integration policies and related multi-level governance mechanisms in Paris. Successful integration benefits both migrants and the receiving society yet takes time and appropriate measures. In particular, the implementation of multi-sectoral policy requires coordination arrangements among different levels of government and the variety of actors involved.

There are diverse, complementary dimensions of migrant integration in host-societies which require the involvement of a multitude of policy fields (e.g. access to the labour market, housing, education, social, cultural, etc.) (Schnapper, 2007; OECD, 2014). Integration is also understood as a two-way process which concerns both people with migration backgrounds and the society as a whole, and hence integration is not only about a specific population but also about the response and inclusiveness of the receiving society (Schnapper, 2007; Schnapper, 2008). Indeed, integration encompasses dimensions, “dialectical relationships”, between the receiving society and minority and migrant groups (Simon and Tiberj, 2012).

A central tenet of this report is the focus on multi-level governance. An effective multi-level governance of public policies depends on the relations among public actors at different levels of government (vertical), but also within the involved administrations (up and low horizontal) (Charbit, 2011). A coordinated public action for migrant integration policies and programs, including with non-governmental actors, is an essential component to achieve the desired outcomes of the policy, so the need to work together for local integration of migrants and refugees (OECD, 2018).

Migration has traditionally been approached as a national prerogative considered emblematic of national sovereignty and the State capacity for border control (Giraudon, 2009). On the other hand, tasks related to migrant integration are often layered at various levels of government (Scholten and Penninx, 2016). Local authorities, who are at the forefront in providing essential services for migrant and vulnerable migrant groups, have taken an essential role in the design and implementation of responses favouring migrant integration. Indeed, it is at the local level that integration takes place and where positive and negative aspects of coexistence in diversity are experienced (Scholten, 2014).

Paris counts on historical experience as a migration hub and as other European cities mobilised its services proactively responding to the 2015 increase of arrivals of humanitarian migrants. The multi-level character of migrant integration has to be understood in the increased decentralisation in France, which started in the 1980s and continued throughout the 2000s with latest territorial organisation reforms in 2015-17.

The following case study about the city of Paris (France) is organised in two sections. A first section is a snapshot of migration in the city including stock, historic migration waves, nationalities and refugee flows. The legal framework is outlined and the main challenges emerging today in the city related to migrant integration are discussed. The second part presents the responses to migrant integration in Paris. A specific attention is given to the identification of the relevant institutions and the multi-level governance mechanisms for migrant integration. These actions are presented according to the objectives identified in the OECD "Checklist for Public Action to Migrant integration at the Local Level" (OECD, 2018a). The first block of the Checklist presents the multi-level governance setting that applies to Paris's integration policy; the institutional mapping helps to clarify the allocation of competences across levels of government. The second block describes how integration solutions are designed over time and aim to create close interaction among all groups. The third block overviews operational, capacity building and monitoring tools used by the city for policy implementation. The last block introduces sectoral actions to facilitate integration through the labour market, education, housing and social services.

Chapter 1. Migration Snap-shot of the city of Paris

1.1. Migration insights: National and local level flows, stock and legal framework

Official statistical data on the presence of migrants use three categories: immigrants, foreign nationals and native-born individuals with at least one parent who is a migrant. According to the most recent INSEE data, immigrant (i.e. individuals born foreign in a foreign country who might have obtained French nationality) represented on January 2014, 8.9% of the population in France (Brutel, 2016; OECD, 2017b). While there has been evolution in the countries of origin in the past 45 years, the main countries remain Italy, Spain, Portugal, Algeria and Morocco. France has a long history of international migration and the presence of migrants today results from several migration inflows from the 20th century. Between the two world wars, workers from Spain and Italy arrived in the country responding to the needs of the expanding industrial and agricultural sectors. After 1945, the reconstruction efforts particularly important in the most populated urban areas, called for workers from colonial Algeria, first, and other Maghreb areas after. They were followed from the 1960s by Portuguese and sub-Saharan Africa nationals, and by the end of the century arrivals of Asian migrants coming mainly from Turkey and China (Brutel, 2016). In 1968, there was a strong concentration of economic activity in the Île-de France region which accounted for, at that time, 40% of the industrial work and 30% of the French population. Consistently, 50% of immigrants settled in Île-de France. Yet, while industrial labour has been declining since the 1970s, especially in these areas, the immigrant population is still highly concentrated in these zones (Brutel, 2016).

Foreign-born represented in 2017 12.3% of France population. The rate of foreign-born over total population is lower in France compared to the OECD average (13.1%) and to other EU peers: in Germany foreign-born represent 15.4% of the population, in Belgium 16.7, in Austria 18.9% and in Switzerland 29.5% (OECD, 2018[1]).

While the population of foreign residents is smaller than in other European countries and France is close to the EU-27 average in terms of migrant population, the role of France as receiver of migrants throughout the 20th century means that France has a large second-generation migrant population, which is tracked by the INSEE through the "descendants of migrants" category (*descendants d'immigrés*). In 2008, France was the EU-27 country with the highest percentage of descendants of migrants (Bouvier, 2012). In 2015, 7.3 million people (11% of the population) born in France had at least one immigrant parent. Among them, 45% are of European origin, 31% from the Maghreb (i.e. Northern African), 11% Sub-Saharan Africa, 9% Asia, 4% America and Oceania (Brutel, 2017). Descendants of migrants are not as geographically clustered as immigrants: 30% of descendants of migrants live in the urban area of Paris (Brutel, 2017).

1.1.1. The urban area of Paris as a migration hub

The distribution of migrants across the territory is highly concentrated. According to the INSEE, 90% of migrants having arrived in the country in the past five years live in large urban areas (Brutel, 2016). The geographic localisation of recently arrived migrants follows the existing distribution, as areas which received the first migration inflows remained the main destinations for incoming migration arrivals (Noiriel, 2002; Safi, 2009). According to the national statistics institute (INSEE), the concentration of migrants is higher than the one of non-migrants: while nine out of ten migrants live in urban areas spaces, this is the case for eight out of ten non-migrants (Safi, 2009; Diaz-Ramirez, Liebig, Thoreau and Veneri, 2018).

The city of Paris has a long history of attracting foreigners. As a European hub, Paris has the most diverse population in France with more than 150 nationalities represented in the city. According to INSEE data, while the Île-de-France region hosts around 20% of the total population in France, 40% of migrants present in mainland France reside in this region. A third of migrants arrived in the past five years live in Île-de-France. (Brutel, 2016; OECD, 2017b).

15% of Paris population has a foreign nationality and 20% is foreign born (among which more than a third have acquired French nationality). The most common nationalities are Algeria, China, Portugal, Morocco and Italy.

1.1.2. Migration legislative framework

According to French legislation[1], non EU-foreign residents are required to obtain a residence permit: either (1) the temporary residence permit *(Carte de séjour temporaire)* which is the first residence permit that a foreigner receives and lasts for a year , (2) the pluri-annual residence card *(Carte de séjour pluriannuelle)* for a maximum length of four years addressed to foreigners who have already been admitted in France and only delivered after a first residence permit, (3) the resident card which is valid for 10 years and renewable, (4) the permanent resident card which is the completion of the integration path and allows the foreigner to live and work in France without renewing a residence permit. There are long delays to obtain administrative appointments for the residence permit which leads to repetitive deliverance of "*récépissés*", temporarily substituting for the residence permits (Vandendriessche, 2012). For a complete presentation of the OECD's work on recent legislative changes in France, refer to « *Le recrutement des travailleurs immigrés en France* » (OECD, 2017b).

1.1.3. Recent inflows of asylum seekers and refugees

Like in many other European contexts, the number of asylum seekers and refugees has sharply increased since 2015. In 2015, the number of first-time asylum applications climbed sharply with a 25.5% surge, to 75 000 applications. The growth continued in 2016, reaching the highest peak in French history with 79 000 first-time applications (OECD, 2017a). Most asylum seekers were from Sudan, Afghanistan, Haiti, Albania, Syria, Democratic Republic of Congo and Guinea (OECD, 2017a). France granted international protection to around 43 000 people in 2017 through refugee or subsidiary protection status. Overall, the OFPRA accepts 29% of first instance requests, a figure which climbs up to 38% when including successful appeals before the National Court of Asylum Rights.

Figure 1.1. Asylum applicants in France, 2008-2016

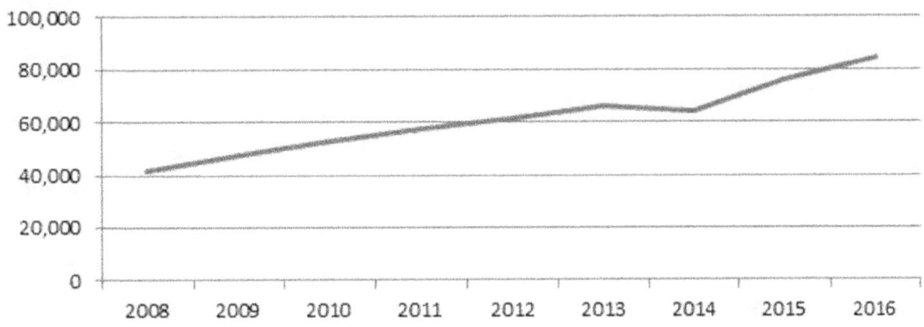

100,000
80,000
60,000
40,000
20,000
0
2008 2009 2010 2011 2012 2013 2014 2015 2016

Source: Eurostat.

1.1.4. Asylum legislative framework

French asylum legislation has evolved since 2014 and further details are given in Annex C.

A 2015 reform granted new rights to asylum seekers (e.g. automatically suspends decisions after appeals have been heard by the National Court of Asylum CNDA) and sped up the process of application with a target to process asylum applications on average of nine months by the end of 2016. Yet according to numbers provided by the Ministry of Interior, in 2016 the procedure lasted 14 months. In February 2018, a new Asylum bill was proposed by the national government engaged in reducing the asylum registration process, instruction and judgment phases. It aims to reduce to six months the length of instruction of asylum demands (appeal included), which would especially concern Île-de-France where the concentration of asylum seekers makes the procedure longer. It also aims to reduce from 120 to 90 days the registration time once the migrant has entered France, and the time available for appealing a rejection (from a month to 15 days)[2]. This law was being debated at the time of publication; therefore, its final characteristics cannot be presented here.

1.1.5. Distribution of asylum seekers and refugees in France

Over the past two years, Paris has experienced an increase in the arrivals of humanitarian migrants like many other urban centres in Europe. Île-de-France receives around 40% of spontaneous arrival inflows of asylum seekers in the national territory. Out of the 63 649 asylum requests made in 2016 in France, 24 020 were submitted in the region of Île-de-France, including almost half of them in the city of Paris (10 151) (OFPRA, 2017).

Preliminary observations on the location of asylum seekers gathered by the OECD in 2017 identify that the number of asylum seekers hosted in accommodation facilities by the national government is higher in the regions of Grand-Est and Auvergne-Rhone-Alpes than in Île-de-France, illustrating the efforts of the government to spread reception pressure from the capital region to other parts of the country (see 4.1.4) (Proietti and Veneri, 2017).

At the regional level, Île-de-France is the biggest third region in terms of the number of hosted asylum seekers in the accommodation system, from preliminary observations gathered in 2017 (Proietti and Veneri, 2017).

Figure 1.2. Hosted asylum seekers in the accommodation system by region

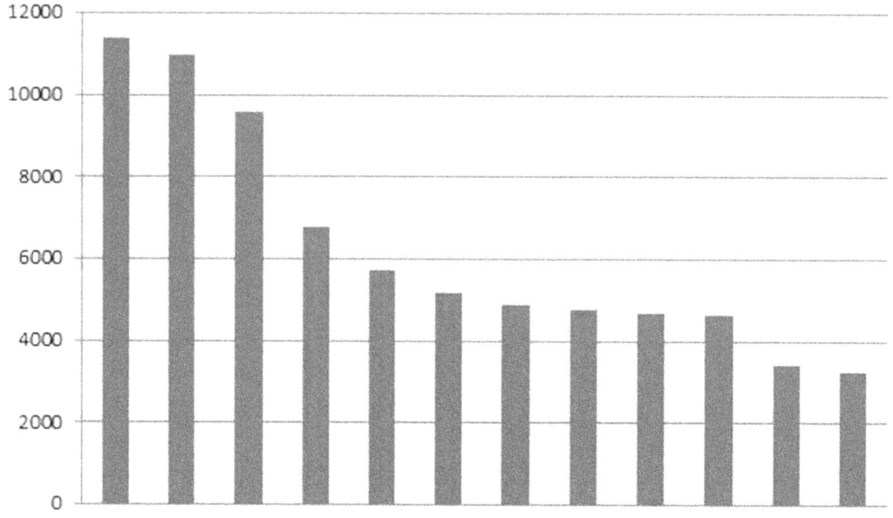

Source: Proietti, P. and P. Veneri (2017), "The location of hosted asylum seekers across regions and cities", paper presented at the 31st OECD Working Party on Territorial Indicators, May 2017.

In France, there is a relatively high concentration of asylum seekers in urban areas (See Figure 1). While the number of municipalities in France is the highest across the OECD (above 36 000), only a small percentage of the municipalities (less than 5%) were hosting asylum seekers at the beginning of 2017. In the city of Paris, there were 3 907 asylum seekers hosted in accommodation centres in 2017 (AT-SA; CADA; HUDA) (see Section 2.1.4).

Figure 1.3. Absolute numbers of people hosted in France inside and outside Functional Urban Areas

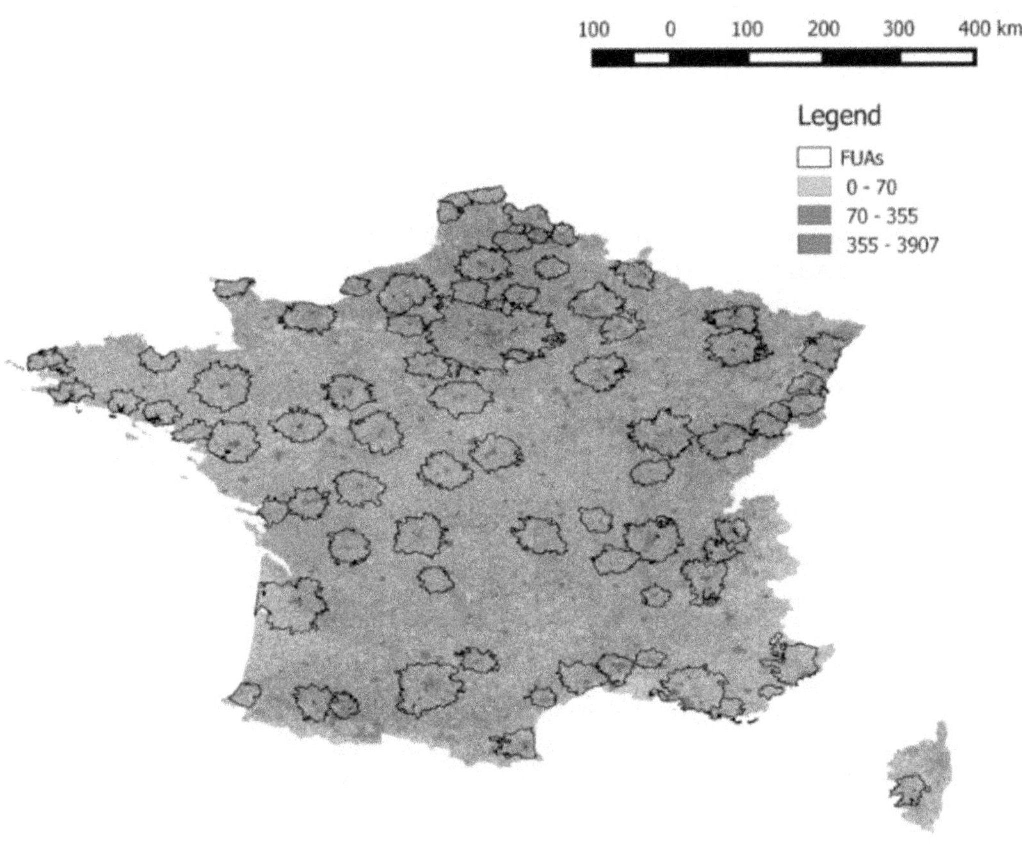

Note: The OECD definition of Functional Urban Areas uses population density to identify urban cores and travel-to-work flows to identify the hinterlands whose labour market is highly integrated with the cores.
Source: Proietti and Veneri (2017).

Migrants accounted for 76% of the total homeless population in Paris in 2015 (APUR, 2017a). In July 2017, 2 700 migrants lived in the streets of Paris. Since 2015, the media has reported the presence of newly arrived persons who gather in Parisian street camps in specific neighbourhoods such as La Chapelle, La Villette and Boulevard Stalingrad. Most irregular migrant street camps are located in the Northeast area of the city, the areas which has historically had a higher share of migrants. Since 2017, following the 2016 evacuation of the Calais camp, several NGOs have highlighted further increases in the presence of homeless migrants in Paris. As of March 2018, the asylum-related NGO France Terre d'Asile which undertakes *maraudes*[3] to identify and support homeless migrants, has counted 1 885 migrants living in street camps made of tents (400 in Canal Saint Martin and 1 400 in Quai du Lot and Quai de l'Allier in the northern border between Paris and the neighbouring city of Saint Denis) (Baumard, 2018)[4]. Some of them fall within the Dublin protocol and thus cannot directly access the French asylum procedure. Some cannot access shelter facilities because of lack of capacity. Following the government strategy, the Police Prefecture is in charge of sheltering those migrants who are "a priori" asylum seekers. In the first semester of 2017, the Paris prefecture (information collected by the OECD during field interviews) had conducted 70 evacuation operations and transferred future asylum seekers from the spontaneous camps to emergency humanitarian centres (100 CHU present in Île-de France). Once filed their asylum request, asylum seekers would be transferred to a reception centre (CADA) during the application procedure (see more details in Section 2.1.4). Some NGOs reported that this method does not eliminate the formation of other camps.

1.2. City Well-being and inclusion

The following section will introduce some integration outcomes while describing the residential and economic characteristics of the city.

The OECD measure of well-being in regions[5] (TL2 level) shows that income inequalities across French regions are larger than in Germany but smaller than in the United Kingdom: households' adjusted disposable income is 40% higher in Île-de-France than in Nord-Pas-de-Calais. (OECD, 2016b).

In the region of Île-de-France (TL2), in which Paris is situated, well-being is quite different from the average well-being. Île-de-France is performing better in the accessibility to services, health, jobs and income. Instead, Île-de-France is a slightly worse performer in education, safety, life satisfaction and sense of community and among the worse in civic engagement, housing and environment (ad-hoc analysis based on OECD well-being dataset 2017).

Figure 1.4. Well-being in Île-de-France, 2017

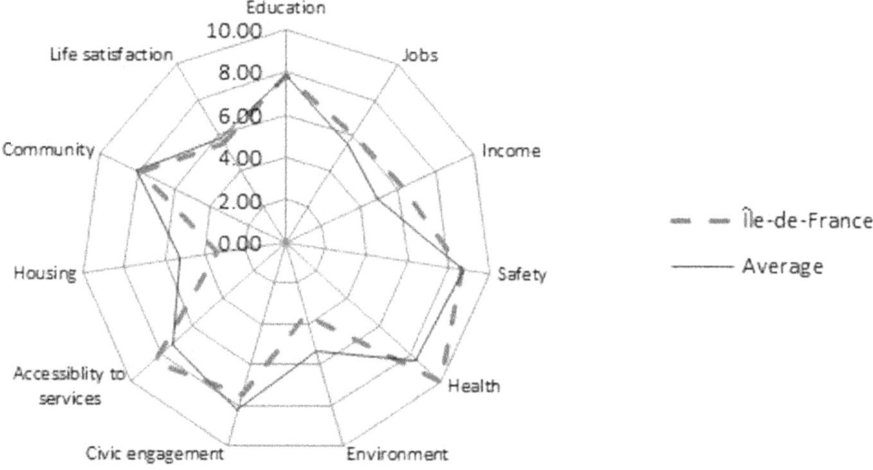

Note: Further information can be found at www.oecdregionalwellbeing.org/FR10.html.
Source: Ad-hoc elaboration on well-being dataset on Île-de-France region (2017).

1.2.1. A dynamic European hub with a strong economy

Paris is the economic and political capital of France, and the most populous city: 2 220 445 inhabitants. The Parisian region *(Île-de-France)* comprises 12 million people. According to Paris region data, it has the highest GDP in the European Union in terms of value generation, accounting for 30.3% of France's GDP, and 4.5% of the EU's GDP (Paris Region, 2018).

Paris is an attractive city with the highest employment rate in France. The Parisian territory is a dense and dynamic economic fabric that is able to create employment in leading recruiting sectors. Paris fared better during the economic crisis than the overall national territory and its employment area has a considerable potential with 34 000 jobs (Mairie de Paris, 2015a). Paris is an attractive territory for companies. 600 companies are created every week and there are more than 367 322 active companies (Mairie de Paris, 2015a)

White collar, executive and senior intellectual jobs are increasing. The city hosts the French and/or European headquarters of several international corporations. It is also an academic and research and development centre with several institutions of higher learning that attract a diverse student body from Europe and other countries. The economic attractiveness of the city was reinforced when the world's biggest start-up campus - Station F - was inaugurated in 2017 (https://stationf.co/). Further, Paris is the world's most popular tourist destination.

Paris is globally attractive and competitive but these economic transformations led to an increasing dual structure in which low skilled immigrant and foreign residents cannot access the increasingly knowledge intensive labour market and high added value employment opportunities (Lelévrier et al., 2017).

1.2.2. Segregation patterns in the city

Socioeconomic disparities and spatial segregation are sharp in Paris. Recent OECD research has shown that the French capital has one of the highest income inequalities relative to its population, on par with cities such as San Francisco (OECD, *Making cities work for all*, 2016; OECD, *Divided cities*, 2018). The metropolitan area of Greater Paris has the highest income inequalities among French metropolises (APUR, 2017b). Within the metropolitan area, it is in the city of Paris where income inequalities are wider: after redistribution the income of the more affluent households is 6.6 times higher than the income of the poorest households (APUR, 2017b).

Unemployment rates vary across the districts of Paris. The highest share of unemployed and economically-deprived individuals is concentrated in neighbourhoods in the east and north and some clusters in the southern districts. In contrast, there is a considerably low unemployment rate in the affluent central and western districts and in most parts of the city's south. Intermediate districts, north of the river Seine, bridge between these contrasting areas (UCL INEQ-CITIES Atlas, 2017).

Similarly, beneficiaries of the government's minimum allowances are concentrated in the same north eastern districts. The 18th, 19th and 20th arrondissements account for 38% of Paris' welfare beneficiaries yet they account for only 26% of the active population of the city (Mairie de Paris, 2015a based on INSEE RP 2012). Social housing distribution across the city of Paris is highly uneven. Today, social housing is concentrated in three districts: almost 50% of the total social housing stock is in two -northeast arrondissements (19th and 20th) and a southern district (13th) (APUR, 2017c).

In the city of Paris there are twenty Priority districts targeted by the national government through the City Policy (see box 2.2), located mainly in the east and north (13th, 18th, 19th and 20th arrondissements but also in the 10th, 11th 14th and 17th). The choice of the neighbourhoods is based on the single criterion of poverty concentration. These districts reflect high levels of economic deprivation, 26% of residents in area targeted by the city policy live below the low-income threshold, versus the Paris average of 11% (APUR, 2016a).

Migrants are concentrated in the outer districts and neighbouring municipalities of Greater Paris. Since 1968, the concentration of the immigrant population within Île-de-France and particularly Paris' urban area has increased (Safi, 2009). According to 2007, INSEE data, the spatial concentration of migrants in Paris has been accelerating with the share of migrants rising in the areas where migrant presence was already the strongest in 1999. Other factors influencing the choice of the neighbourhood are the lower housing costs and the higher availability of social housing. INSEE data shows that the migrant population is more present in the Northeast Parisian Arrondissements (e.g. 18th, 19th, 20th) and neighbouring municipalities (i.e. Saint-Denis, La Courneuve, Gennevilliers, Bobigny). In fact, Eric Lejoindre, Mayor of the 18th Arrondissement, an area in which migration has a great impact, invited at an OECD event in April 2018 stated that his district is and has historically been a "land of welcome". In Parisian City Policy districts (see Figure 1.5), 30% of residents are foreign, while on average migrants represent 20% of the city population (APUR, 2016a). Concentration per nationality differs: African migrants' concentration (Maghreb and Sub-Saharan Africa) has increased whereas Spanish and Italian immigrant tended to disperse (Safi 2009 based on INSEE population census).

Figure 1.5. Migrant population in Paris and City-Policy neighbourhoods

Source: Apur (2016a), *Les quartiers Parisiens de la politique de la ville - Contrat de ville 2015-2020.*

Table 1.1. Socio-economic indicators by Arrondissement, Paris

Arrondissement	Migrant population (%) (2012)	Foreign population (%) (2012)	Median Disposable Income in € by UC (2012)	Unemployed (%) (2013)	Welfare (RSA) beneficiaries (%) (2013)	Social housing (%) (2014)
I	18	13.4	32 220	13.1	4.6	9.4
II	21.7	16.8	28 620	14.7	4.2	5.5
III	20.5	16.5	29 798	14.2	4.7	6.6
IV	19.1	14.8	30 164	14.6	4.3	12.4
V	17	12.9	32 359	10.9	2.9	8.2
VI	16.2	12.4	39 218	10.8	2.6	3
VII	19.7	16.3	42 250	9.5	2.3	1.4
VIII	20	15.1	40 671	11.3	3.6	3
IX	16.9	12.6	31 864	14.7	4.5	6.1
X	22.9	18.3	23 695	18.1	6.9	12.7
XI	18.8	14	25 239	17	6.7	12.7
XII	15.9	10.7	26 297	14.8	6.9	19.9
XIII	21.6	13.9	22 759	14.7	6	35.5
XIV	20	14.8	26 613	13.2	4	24.8
XV	18.1	13.1	30 137	11.3	3.4	16.4
XVI	20.9	15.1	39 060	10.6	3	3.8
XVII	19	14	29 032	13.3	4.5	12.4
XVIII	23.4	18.4	19 896	19.8	8.1	20.6
IXX	25.5	17.9	18 335	22.1	9.4	38
XX	21.8	15	19 734	20	8	32.7

Note: See further information at www.apur.org/dataviz/fiches_arrdt/index.html.
Source: Data aggregated based on « APUR Portraits d'arrondissements », INSEE census; DADS, Filosofi CAF de Paris, Olap, Inventaire SRU, ville de Paris, Cnaf, Pôle emploi, Apur.

Figure 1.6. Migrant population rates in the Île-de-France region

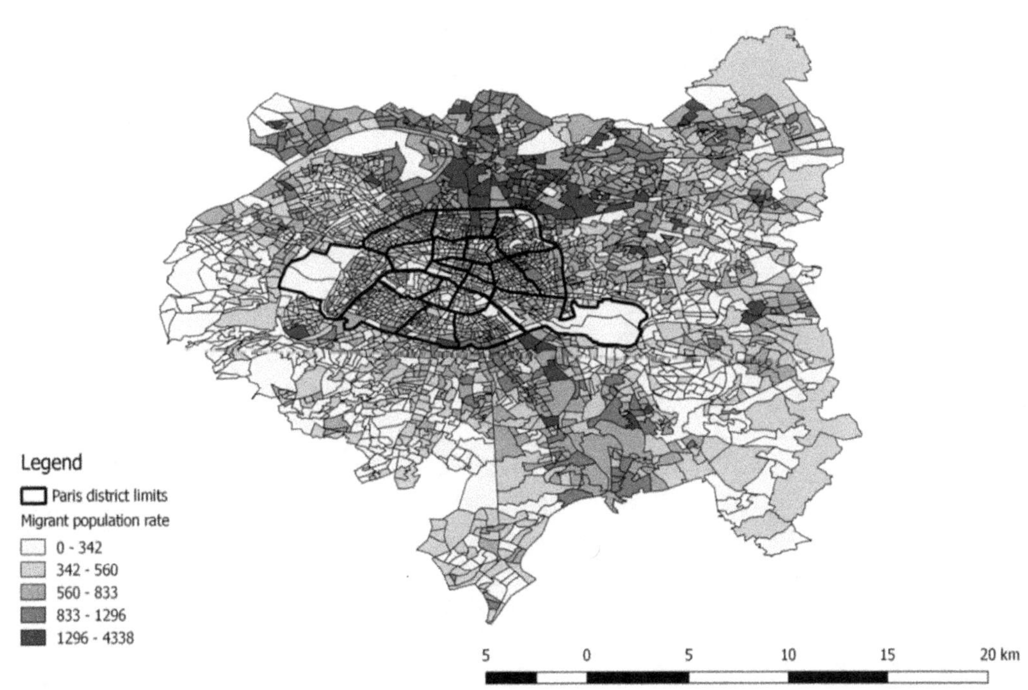

Source: Authors' elaboration from APUR data available at http://opendata.apur.org/datasets/iris-demographie.

1.2.3. Public opinion and perception of migrants

The increasing arrivals of vulnerable migrants to the city in 2015 triggered a large solidarity wave from the Parisian society. However, the Parisian and French population remains divided with regard to migrants. A 2016 IFOP study illustrates, that the Parisian and French population tends to be sceptical of migrants and especially asylum applicants. Only 33% of Parisian interviewees (national average 27%) believe migrants arriving in France have an economic or financial potential and 59% of Parisians (national average 61%) believe that there is an overall lack of capacity in France to welcome additional new arrivals (IFOP, 2016). Migrants remain a dividing issue within the French society at large, with an August 2016 IPSOS survey indicating that 57% of French respondents think that there are too many immigrants in the country, and only 11% deem migration to have a positive impact on the country (IPSOS, 2016). Furthermore, research conducted by the Pew Research Centre in 2016 across the EU showed that only 26% of French people think that diversity makes their country a better place to live, and highlights scepticism amongst a wide share of the population that migrants can truly integrate (Pew Research Centre, 2016).

Notes

1. Code de l'entrée et du séjour des étrangers et du droit d'asile.
2. Further information about asylum legislation can be found at: https://es.scribd.com/document/368911950/Presentation-des-dispositions-du-projet-de-loi-asile-immigration#from_embed.
3. "Maraudes" are undertaken by NGOs on a regular basis. They are walks throughout Paris to identify and count vulnerable residents in the streets and provide them with social support.
4. Updated information on the evolution of street camps in Paris can be found in: http://www.lemonde.fr/journaliste/maryline-baumard/.

Chapter 2. The Checklist for public action to migrant integration at the local level applied to the city of Paris

This section is structured following the Checklist for public action to migrant integration at the local level, (OECD, 2018a) which comprises a list of 12 key evidence-based objectives, articulated into four mini blocks that can be used by policy makers and practitioners in the development and implementation of migrant integration programmes, at local, regional, national and international levels. This Checklist highlights for the first time common messages and cross-cutting lessons learnt around policy frameworks, institutions, and mechanisms that feature in policies for migrant and refugee integration.

This innovative tool has been elaborated by the OECD as part of the larger study on "Working Together for Local Integration of Migrants and Refugees" supported by the European Commission, Directorate General for Regional and urban policies. This part gives a description of the actions implemented in Paris following this framework.

Box 2.1. A checklist for public action to migrant integration at the local level

Block 1. Multi-level governance: Institutional and financial settings

- Objective 1. Enhance effectiveness of migrant integration policy through improved vertical co-ordination and implementation at the relevant scale.
- Objective 2. Seek policy coherence in addressing the multi-dimensional needs of, and opportunities for, migrants at the local level.
- Objective 3. Ensure access to, and effective use of, financial resources that are adapted to local responsibilities for migrant integration.

Block 2. Time and space: Keys for migrants and host communities to live together

- Objective 4. Design integration policies that take time into account throughout migrants' lifetimes and evolution of residency status.
- Objective 5. Create spaces where the interaction brings migrant and native-born communities closer.

Block 3. Local capacity for policy formulation and implementation

- Objective 6. Build capacity and diversity in civil service, with a view to ensure access to mainstream services for migrants and newcomers.
- Objective 7. Strengthen co-operation with non-state stakeholders, including through transparent and effective contracts.
- Objective 8. Intensify the assessment of integration results for migrants and host communities and their use for evidence-based policies.

Block 4. Sectoral policies related to integration

- Objective 9. Match migrant skills with economic and job opportunities.
- Objective 10. Secure access to adequate housing.
- Objective 11. Provide social welfare measures that are aligned with migrant inclusion.
- Objective 12. Establish education responses to address segregation and provide equitable paths to professional growth.

Source: Authors' elaboration.

2.1. Block 1: Multi-level governance: Institutional and financial setting

2.1.1. Objective 1: Enhance effectiveness of migrant integration policy through improved vertical co-ordination and implementation at the relevant scale

Governance setting: France's decentralisation process

France was historically built as a unitary state with a centralised organisation around Paris. Since the 1980s, a series of institutional reforms have allocated more autonomy to subnational governments, through a process of decentralisation. Competences are allocated to three tiers of subnational government, which are: (1) Regions, (2) Departments and (3) Communes and, along with a strong national government, yet in practice these competences tend to be complementary and not exclusively under the responsibility of a single government level (Verpeaux, 2015). In addition, there is no "*tutelle*" (authority rule) from one elected level on another one and the "general competence clause" allows local authorities to exercise competences beyond those formally ascribed to them. Because of the large number of communes, there is a tradition of inter-municipal cooperation and there are various forms of Public Bodies for Intercommunal cooperation (EPCI) which can have taxation powers. Recent reforms, in particular in 2014-15, developed the "Metropolitan level" of inter-municipality (Verpeaux, 2015; OECD, 2017c; OECD 2017d). Understanding the general organisation of these various levels of government is essential to appreciate the multi-level governance of migrant integration. See 2.4.4.Annex B for a list of competences for each level of government.

In this complex institutional and regulatory landscape - in which the central government still plays a major role but increasingly transfer competences to subnational governments – multi-level governance is essential to coordinate the wide array of highly interdependent actors and institutional structures at multiple levels. Whereas migrant regulation is managed by the National Government and its delegations, key integration domains are handled by subnational governments.

Figure 2.1. General scheme of the multi-layered government setting in Paris

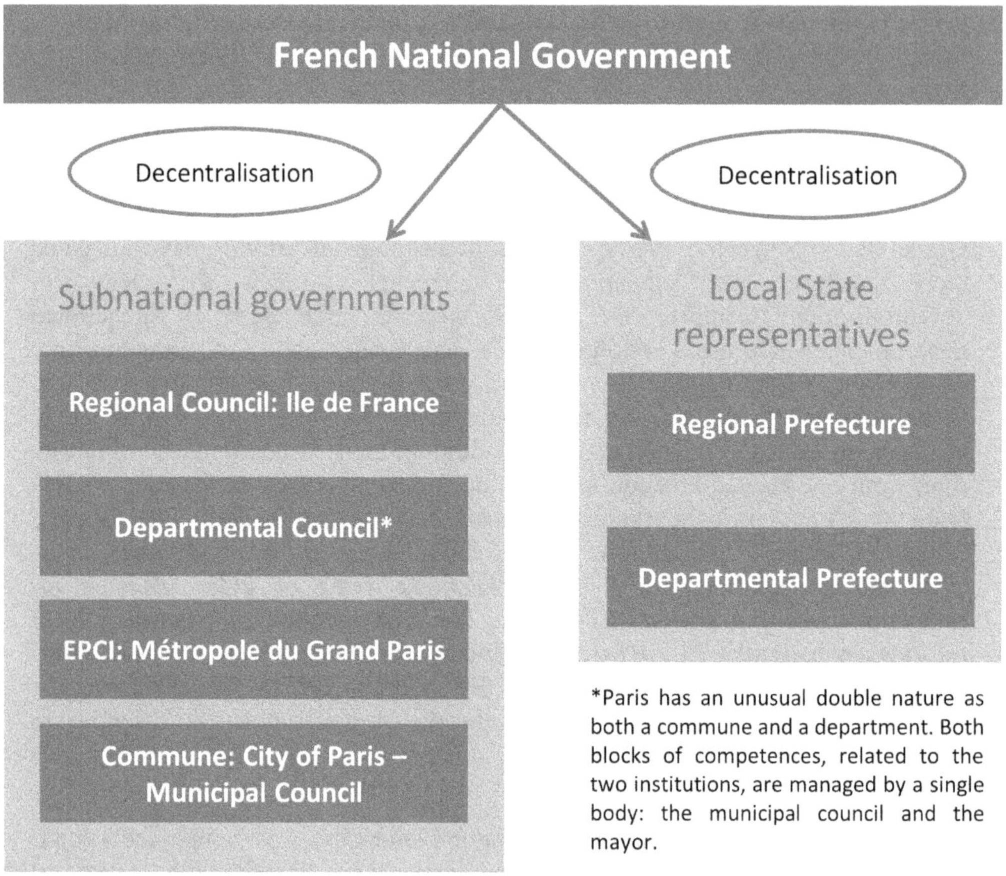

French National Government

Decentralisation

Decentralisation

Subnational governments

Regional Council: Ile de France

Departmental Council*

EPCI: Métropole du Grand Paris

Commune: City of Paris – Municipal Council

Local State representatives

Regional Prefecture

Departmental Prefecture

*Paris has an unusual double nature as both a commune and a department. Both blocks of competences, related to the two institutions, are managed by a single body: the municipal council and the mayor.

Source: Author's elaboration.

National level: Competences for migration and migrant integration

National goals and policy tools for integration

Historically, integration policy in France is based on the Republican principle of Equality (*Égalité*) which translated into social policies of *Droit commun* or General Law in English. This principle, which guides the design and development of public policy in all sectors, is stated in the first article of the Constitution. It underlines equal treatment for all individuals, regardless of race, religion or ethnicity and avoids group-targeted policies (Escalfré-Dublet, 2016).

In practice, French policy-makers did not address migrant integration until the late 1980s. The elaboration of an official definition of French integration was in the 1990s under the lead of the High Council for Integration. The approach remains general: easing access to all groups to universal services rather than creating a specific public policy for migrant integration. Currently there are monitoring and policy tools to act against all forms of discrimination including racism such as the national plan against racism and antisemitism (2018-2020)[1], and an annual report on racism, anti-Semitism, antimuslim and antichristian acts[2].

The only exception to the generic or universal national approach to migrant integration is the Contract of Republican Integration (CRI) for recently arrived migrants. The CIR is the only specific national dispositive for migrant integration. Tested in 2003, rolled out in 2007 and reformulated in 2016, the CRI is an essential tool for the French approach to migrant integration implemented through the OFII (see below). The CRI concerns foreign people having received residence permits for the first time and aiming to live in France. This contractual agreement with the French government establishes an integration path for a length of five years. By signing the CRI at the OFII, migrants commit to uphold French values and learn the language and thus receive free language classes and civic training. After an initial language exam, which determines their level of proficiency, the OFII assigns migrants to language classes delivered by 34 partner language schools and qualified organisations operating across the national territory, not necessarily operating in contact with local authorities. There are three language learning paths based on the initial language level (50-100-200 hours). After the CIR finalisation, the minimal language level theoretically reached is A1. Training attendance and attainment of the A1 level is mandatory in order to have access to the multi-annual residence permits after one year of residence (yet in practice attending at least 80% of the classes and progress between initial and final exam are considered enough). Further, acquiring permanent residence status and then eventually citizenship, should they apply for it, is subject to attaining an A2 language level[3]. Recent OECD research has further analysed national policies for migrant integration in the job market (OECD, 2017b).

Furthermore, a national urban policy - *La politique de la ville* (City Policy) - aims at reducing intra-urban inequalities and improving living conditions in deprived neighbourhoods, which heavily affects migrants as they are over-represented in such zones. This policy concerns 1 500 neighbourhoods in France targeted based on the ratio of low income residents by the "Priority geography". The City Policy aims to enhance universal services with reinforced funding in these specific neighbourhoods and implements targeted initiatives specific to them to bridge inequalities. The City Policy is designed at the national level under the supervision of the Minister of Territorial Cohesion and the General Commission for Territorial Equality (CGET), a service of the Prime Minister, and implemented at the city level by a complex governance structure including different levels of government (prefecture, region, municipality) as well as partner public and non-governmental stakeholders. The relationship between City Policy and migrant integration policies has not been formally clarified (see Box 2.2).

Relevant tools for migrant integration are housing and urban planning. The national government (Minister of Territorial Cohesion) holds essential powers defining national prerogatives in these areas.

Main national institutions with integration-related responsibilities

Currently, at the national level, there is no ministry in charge of migration and integration issues. Between 2007 and 2010, there was a Ministry of Immigration, integration, national identity and cohesive development (*Ministère de l'immigration, de l'intégration, de l'identité nationale et du développement solidaire* (MIIINDS)). There is an institution in charge of monitoring all forms of discrimination including racism, the Inter-ministerial delegation for the fight against racism, antisemitism and anti-LGBT hatred (*Délégation interministérielle à la Lutte contre le racisme, l'antisémitisme et la haine anti-LGBT* (DILCRAH)), which was created in 2014.

In France as in other European countries, the Ministry of Interior oversees immigration issues and population registration, as well as national security matters. Since 2009, the ministry of Interior has also been in charge of the implementation of the Contract of Republican Integration (CRI) addressed to foreign "primo-arrivals" ("recently arrived" meaning the five years after foreign residents arrive in the country). The DGEF (*Direction générale des étrangers en France)* manages foreign resident matters, including reception and integration. Within the DGEF, there are three directorates: the directorate of immigration, the directorate of asylum and the directorates of reception, accompaniment and nationality (DAEEN). The DGEF prepares and executes the national budgetary programs "104-Integration" and "303-Asylum and Immigration". Between 2017 and 2018, the national budget under the programme "Integration and Access to the French nationality" increased from EUR 240 million to EUR 283 million.

The central government maintains an important role at the regional and department levels through deconcentrated delegations of the national administration. State representatives are appointed by the President of the Republic at the regional level (*préfets*) and Department level (*sous-préfet*). Prefects play a crucial role as they coordinate and locally head public services delivered by the central government at the regional level, and manage public safety. They also have the task of controlling the legality and report abuse of regulations by subnational governments.

The *Office français pour l'intégration des immigrés* (OFII), implements the asylum and integration policy managed by the DGEF. The OFII is composed of a central administration in Paris and 31 territorial offices dispersed across the national territory. The OFII is an administrative public body under the supervision of the Ministry of Interior responsible for: (1) the management of regular migration procedures along with prefectures; (2) the management of the Republican Integration Contract (CIR) in partnership with external providers of language courses; (3) the reception and support of asylum seekers. For migrants with a residence permit, the OFII accompanies them through the signature of the CIR. It evaluates their language level and assigns them to language courses. The OFII delivers a two-day compulsory civic training programme to CIR signatories. With regard to asylum seekers, the OFII coordinates and manages the National Reception Initiative (*Dispositif national d'accueil* – DNA), meaning it is responsible for directing them to the temporary accommodation to which they are entitled and allocating the economic allowance specific for asylum seekers (ADA) (See 2.1.4). If their asylum request is accepted, the OFII deploys its traditional role for the integration of recently arrived migrants through the signature of the CIR.

The *Office français de protection des réfugiés et apatrides* (OFPRA) is a French autonomous public establishment which is affiliated with the Ministry of the Interior. It administrated the right to asylum in France, in accordance with international agreements. As a Public Administrative Establishment, the OFPRA enjoys functional autonomy. The headquarters are in the region of Paris with 800 agents. During the debate surrounding the 2015 reform of immigration law, the legislator considered deconcentrating the services of the OFPRA. However, this option was declined for financial and logistical reasons. Nevertheless, the OFPRA conducts missions at the local level, upon the request of Prefects, to inform and train personnel at the Prefectures regarding the asylum procedures. It emerged from OECD interviews with the OFII, that housing solutions for refugees after the temporary shelter offered during the asylum request period is the main issue that arises during these missions.

At the regional level: Île-de-France

The Île-de-France Prefecture is the delegated authority of the central state in the Île-de-France region and oversees a large set of public services delivered by the national government at local level. There is one single Prefecture for the Île-de-France region and the department of Paris. Among other services the Île-de-France Prefecture, and in particular its Direction DRIHL (*Direction régionale et interdepartementale de l'hébergement et du logement*) is responsible for housing and temporary accommodation in Île-de-France. Under the authority of the prefect through the DRIHL, the Integrated Services of Welcome and Integration (SIAO-*Services integrés de l'accueil et de l'intégration*), which is managed by the Samu Social of Paris, manages emergency shelters and centralises both demands and offers of available spaces in department shelters in order to direct users to appropriate structures.

In addition to the prefecture, the State is also represented through the Police Prefecture for all matters regarding security and territorial integrity in the Paris Department and three other departments in Île-de-France. The Police Prefecture is the direct partner of the city in all operations that concern public security and population registration. The Police Prefecture is also responsible for delivering residence permits (identity cards, residence permits, naturalisations, etc.).

Regions were created in 1982 as a new intermediary government level between the national and the department levels, the regional layer in France does not have legislative powers and its administrative capacities are assigned by the State (OECD, 2017a). Regions levy taxes and receive fiscal transfers from the national government to develop their competences, and can also access several EU funds (OECD, 2017a). Recent government reforms have enhanced the regions' responsibilities and reduced the number of regions (apart from overseas) from 22 to 13, while not affecting the Île-de-France or its characteristics.

In France, regions have extensive competence over policy fields such as economic development, environmental protection, research and innovation, and transportation. Due to the size of the Parisian region and its population, Île-de-France benefits from reinforced competences from the national State, especially in the fields of environmental protection, and transportation.

In terms of migrant integration, the regional level has almost no responsibility except for the provision of vocational training, a domain where the region plays a key role since this competence was fully transferred to this level in 2004. Regions organise and finance access to apprenticeships and other professional training programmes for youth and adults through the Public Regional Service of Professional Formation (SPRFP). In the SPRFP framework, regions can address specific groups of people such as illiterate individuals and to coordinate the Validation of Competences (*Validation des acquis de l'expérience*).

Metropolitan level: Paris Métropole (MGP)

The most integrated form of intercommunal body, the "Metropoles", were initiated in 2010 and strongly developed through the MAPTAM law (2014). They only apply to large cities and among them the three major French cities (Paris, Lyon and Marseille), which have a specific status, also in fiscal terms. The Metropolitan area of Paris (MGP) englobes 123 municipalities, among which Paris, and 6.7 million residents. Among its competences are economic, social and cultural development as well as urban planning, housing, "City Policy" and collective services (i.e. water). The creation of this public entity aims at reorganising and sharing public services in the metropolitan area [4]. The metropolitan area is understood as the adequate level to address income-related and territorial inequalities, improve well-being and promote inclusive growth. This recently created actor might be crucial in the coming years, if fully implemented, in bridging the gaps outside of Paris but within the confines of the "metropole" (e.g. La Courneuve, Saint-Denis) and help de-segregate migrant residents through better 'intra-métropole' cooperation (see 1.2). In this context, governance tools such as Territorial Development Contracts have been developed on transport matters (new express subway line) and housing (target to build 70 000 new housing units per year).

In terms of refugee integration, dialogue between the municipal team of Paris and the neighbouring city of Ivry-sur-Seine was crucial to open a humanitarian centre for vulnerable refugee groups (CPA, see Box 2.3). The partnership between both municipalities was essential since the Parisian municipality wanted to use a site owned by Paris located in Ivry to set up this centre. The Parisian municipality points to the example of other cities that have taken similar measures to open humanitarian welcome centres and thus avoid the re-formation of urban camps in the streets of the capital. While for the moment the response has not been positive from neighbouring municipalities, addressing such issues in the context of the MGP could relieve the overcrowded and humanitarian situation in Paris.

Paris as a "commune" and a department

As the capital and biggest city in France, the city of Paris holds, since 1975, a unique place in the French institutional landscape. The city (*ville de Paris*) is both a municipality and a department, a unique case in France, and is responsible for municipal and departmental competences, apart from public safety (the Police Prefecture of Paris holds these powers), which grants the city with more competences and capacities to develop integration than regular French departments or municipalities. The department is considered the "*chef de file*" or lead administration in terms of solidarity measures and social services including welfare economic allowances (deliver the *Revenu de solidarité active,* RSA, which is an economic allowance for residents with insufficient incomes), social protection services (i.e. such as child protection, support to disadvantaged families, elderly and people with disabilities, etc.) and the financial allowances to support housing costs (*Fonds de solidarité pour le logement* – FSL)

Municipalities (*communes*) are the lowest subnational authority and are the most local level of government. They are governed by an elected city council directed by the mayor. Their competences are diversified and include social and health measures through the *Centres communux d'action sociale* CCAS (public entities in charge of social action), building and maintenance of kindergarten and primary schools, culture (i.e. libraries and museums), public spaces and local public safety. EPCI and municipalities have social housing (in collaboration with Social Housing companies, see 2.4.2) and urban planning competences based on national prerogatives.

In terms of integration-relevant matters, the subnational government of Paris, co-shares some responsibilities with higher governmental levels and is fully responsible for others. For instance, co-shares responsibilities with the national government with regards to the implementation of City Policy see section 1.2 (see Box 2.2). A co-shared responsibility is also social housing whose governance is particularly entangled in Île-de-France and Paris (IAU, 2012). The national level oversees national programmes, is in charge of regulatory measures and also owns social housing units in Paris. The city of Paris owns and builds social housing units and allocates housing allowances (FSL). Social housing companies manage social housing units (see 2.4.2). Paris is solely responsible, both as a municipality and as a department, for some sectors that are key for integration such as welfare allocation, social action, cultural and local services, public spaces, etc. Since 2016, Paris has developed specific policies for migrant and refugee reception and integration (see Figure 2.2. for the municipal approach to migrant integration and 2.2.1 for the municipal strategy for refugee reception and integration).

Box 2.2. City Policy in Paris: A multi-level and multi-dimensional place-based policy targeting deprived neighbourhoods

"City Policy" or *Politique de la ville* is a national-urban policy aiming at reducing territorial inequalities, urban segregation and promoting economic, urban and social development in the most disadvantaged areas. It is designed at the national level and jointly implemented with cities at the local level. Over the last forty years and through several reforms (Epstein, 2012), City Policy has specifically targeted several urban districts across the country, selected on the basis of poverty concentration[5]. The policy aims at concentrating public investment (both financial and human) in these districts. The national government shares the responsibility for implementing the policy with subnational governments and non-governmental actors, constituting a complex governance setting. The 5.5 million people living in the 1 500 most disadvantaged neighbourhoods targeted by City Policy represent 9% of French population and 18% of the foreign population in the country benefits from this policy. In a way, City Policy can implicitly be seen as a manner to address migrant integration issues as migrants are overrepresented in these neighbourhoods (Kirszbaum, 2004; Lelevrier et al, 2017).

Since the 1980s, the national institution responsible for City Policy has changed, mirroring its multidimensional character as it involves domains such as unemployment, social cohesion and urban environment. The responsibility now lies with the Ministry of Territorial Cohesion and especially the General Commissariat for Territorial Equality (CGET). The CGET coordinates the line ministries (i.e. Education, Employment, etc.) involved in the implementation while supervising the design, implementation and financing of the policy.

City Policy is executed through the so-called City Contracts (*Contrats de ville*) which are agreed with a participatory process. These contracts represent an example of coordination between levels of government and partner stakeholders that France has tested since decentralisation reforms have aimed to promote cooperation and break down barriers (OECD, 2007; Charbit and Romano, 2017). The City Contract includes three policy objectives: social cohesion, urban renewal and economic development. In Paris, after the 2013 reform streamlining City Policy's categories, 20 priority neighbourhoods were identified on the basis of their low-income level as targeted by City Policy.

The national government is represented in the negotiation of the City contracts by the prefects and the deconcentrated services of the ministries. In Paris, the last and current City Contract was signed on 7 May 2015 and covers the 2015-2020 period. It was signed by the national State (represented by regional prefectures), the regional government (Île-de-France), the education authority in the region (*le Rectorat*), the Paris city government, and several partners, such as local sub-offices of the following national entities: Social Housing providers (*Bailleurs sociaux*), the national Social welfare office for Family allowances Paris (*Caisse d'allocations familiales de Paris*), the National public unemployment office Paris (*Pôle emploi*) as well as the national financial institution for public investment, (*Caisse des dépôts et consignations*). Since the 2014 Lamy Law, the participation of residents is also essential in City Policy in the design of the City Contracts through Neighbourhood Councils. The role of non-governmental actors is essential in Priority Neighbourhoods. The national government has provided EUR 240 million in financing to 7 500 local associations implementing programmes in these neighbourhoods. Through the creation of the "*Entreprises et Quartiers*" charter in 2013, the private sector is incentivised to engage in employing and participating to economic development in these areas. These charters were an initiative of the State and the municipality takes part in it and support several actions regarding employment training, economic development and business creation. For instance, among the projects that fall into this framework are new places dedicated to economic development as part of the "Arc of innovation" programme (e.g. the Python at the gates of the 20th), the development of economic sectors within certain areas such as the support for fashion and design professionals in the Goutte d'Or district or the creation of the Cités Lab in 2017, which are located in districts facing socio-economic difficulties, that offer a diversity of resources and support to residents' entrepreneurship projects (i.e. information, networking, counselling).

Coordination among partners inside the city works as follows. The DPVI (*Département politique de la ville et integration*), which is headed by a deputy mayor, oversees the implementation of the City Contract and works in close coordination with the DU (*Direction de l'urbanisme*) for urban renewal and urban planning purposes. The DPVI has a coordination function and works alongside sectoral departments (DDES for Employment, DASCO social and education affairs). Each priority neighbourhood has a DPVI team coordinating and monitoring the progress of the City Contract. The team is in charge of overseeing municipal activities and allocates funds to local associations operating in the area.

The effectiveness of the City Policy has been highly questioned in France by academic literature and recent OECD research has shed the light on the ongoing segregation in areas which have traditionally been targeted by this policy such as in the Parisian periphery. The *Cour des comptes* identified the lack of national funding and vertical and horizontal coordination as the main bottlenecks for the effectiveness of City Policy. In this context, the financial capacities of the city are essential in the implementation of City Policy.

The financial capacities of the city of Paris allow for further increased allocation of resources to City Policy than in peer cities with lower budgets (i.e. on the outskirts of Paris). In Paris, the city doubles the budget received from the national government for the City Policy (45% from the state and 55% from the city) (Lelevrier et al., 2017). The municipality of Paris acknowledges that the population is younger and there are more migrants in the targeted neighbourhoods of its city policy, so there is a greater need to bolster programmes addressed to these populations (Lelevrier et al., 2017).

The municipal budget for priority neighbourhood programmes comes from both (1) universal sectoral policies which receive one-off funding in these neighbourhoods (86% in 2012) and (2) expenditures specific to the *Contrat de Ville* (14% in 2012). Contrarily to other cities, Paris focuses on the social dimension of City Policy and more resources are allocated to social action (social inclusion and access to employment) than to urban renewal programmes and major urban planning and environment operations. (Lelevrier et al., 2017).

The mid-term evaluation of the Contrat de Ville is in progress with the State and it will be conducted by the APUR (*Atelier parisien d'urbanisme*). The municipality also strives to include its inhabitants in participatory process for evaluating these actions. For this purpose, public meetings are organised in Parisian districts (*arrondisssements*) to give the floor to local actors to report on the city's initiatives and exchange on what has been implemented over the past three years. It also focuses on developing ideas and proposals regarding the needs for upcoming periods.

Source: Author's elaboration.

Evolution of France's integration policies

In February 2018, a parliamentary report (Rapport Taché) commissioned by the Prime Minister was presented in the National Assembly at the same time as the new asylum law. It is called "For an ambitious policy of integration of foreigners arriving in France". The report highlights the lack of holistic integration policy for migrants and provides for a "public policy of integration, ambitious and demanding" through 72 proposals for an integrated migrant integration response at the national level (Taché, 2018).

> *The reports states that* "foreign integration is not recognised today as a public policy per se but is considered the support of migration policy, a subsection of City Policy, an element of the policy to fight discrimination or the specificity of social policies. Its consideration does not tackle the temporal and intergenerational dimension of integration and only applies to the first five years of foreign presence in the national territory" *(*Taché, 2018*)*.

The Taché proposal for a national policy for foreign integration, addresses three key elements: (1) the multidimensional approach to migrant integration; (2) increased policy capacities with further financial capacities for migrant integration; (3) improve and clarify the governance setting of migrant integration with a focus on multi-level and multi-actor governance of migrant integration. The proposal focused on improving the CIR capacities by increasing the supply of language learning courses (including for asylum seekers) along with strengthening migrants' access to employment, education, health housing and social welfare by improving access to rights and services. The report stresses the need to improve the governance of migrant reception and integration policies in France through better horizontal and vertical coordination and highlights the current fragmentation ("*émiettement*") of actors and responsibilities participating in migrant integration as an obstacle to achieving effective migrant integration[6]. Two key proposals of the Taché Report (2018) in terms of governance for the proposed migrant integration are (1) the establishment of an Inter-Ministerial Integration Committee in charge of elaborating and following a strategic pluriannual plan for integration which would encompass the multi-dimensional needs of migrant integration; and (2) the close collaboration with subnational governments, the private sector and the civil society in the design, governance, implementation and evaluation of its efficiency. Interaction with neighbour municipalities can enable the authorities to reach effective scale in social infrastructure and service delivery to migrant and refugees. A first inter-ministerial council – *Comité interministériel á l'intégration* CII- met on June 5th 2018 to approve the action plan containing the measures adopted among the 72 proposals (Comité interministériel á l'intégration, 2018[2]), some of them will be discussed in details in Section 2.4.1. Figure 2.2 represents the institutional mapping of migrant and refugees' integration in Paris, in the context of the allocation of responsibilities across and within levels of government. NGOs that play a key role are also included.

Figure 2.2. Institutional mapping for migrant integration in Paris

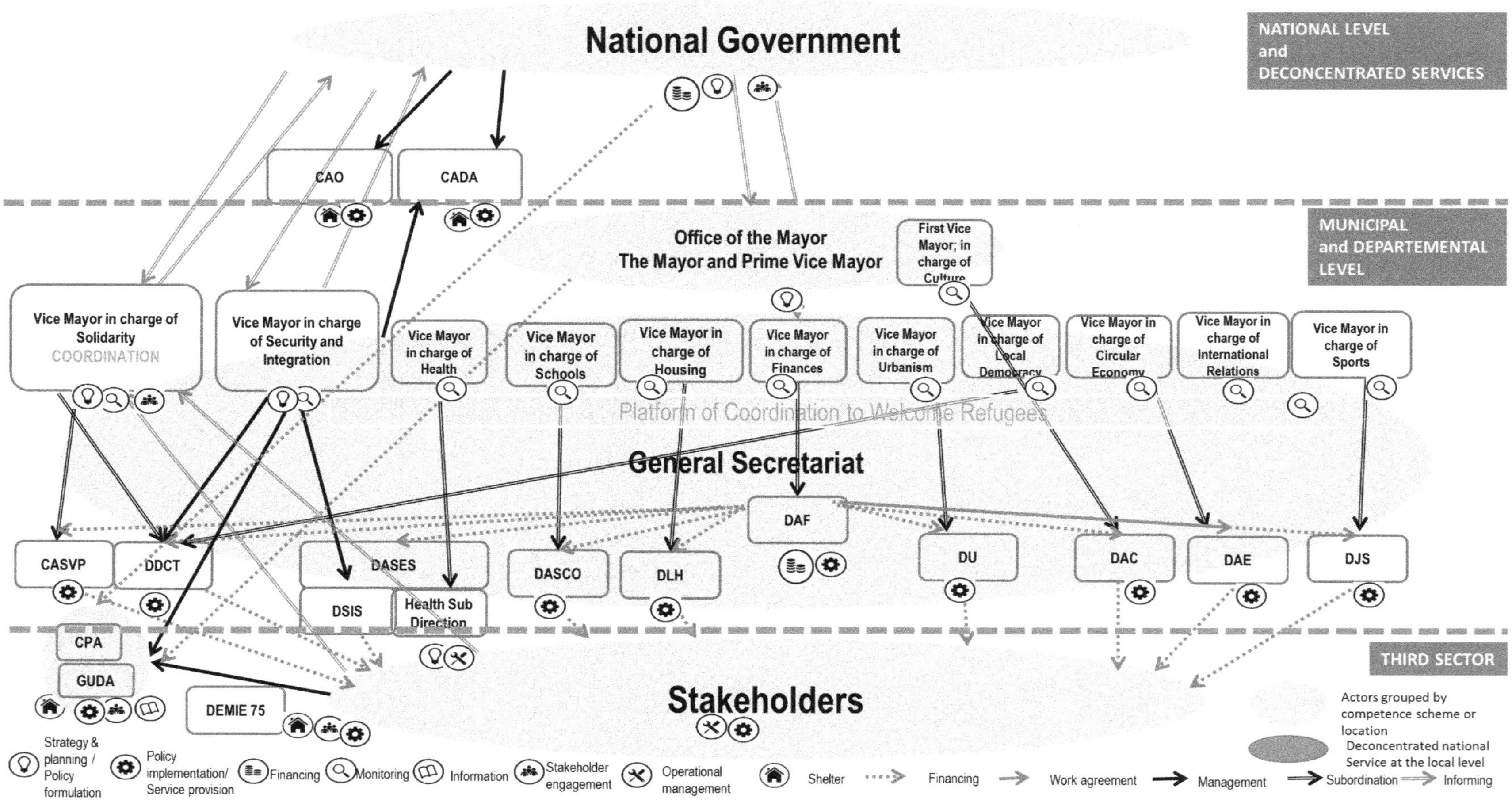

Source: Authors' elaboration.

2.1.2. Objective 2: Seek policy coherence in addressing multi-dimensional migrant needs at the local level

Approach to integration and inclusion policies at the city level

> *"I want to promote the Fraternity Paris by an active fight against discrimination. Paris is a global city of immigration and mixing of cultures. All different, we remain all Parisian. While recognising individual identities, we need to build an inclusive collective identity"- Paris Mayor (2014) Note addressed to Hélène Bidard, Vice-Mayor of Equality between women and men, "the fight against discriminations and human rights".*[7]

Paris integration strategy goes beyond ensuring equal access to public services. Paris is engaged in changing the mentality of its citizens to make them appreciate the benefits of living in a more diverse society. For instance, Paris aims at implementing actions to influence employers such a diversity charter signed by 252 000 Parisian enterprises, obtain a "Diversity label" (AFNOR) and engage reflections on the recruitment and career management criteria for municipal staff.

To make universal services accessible for all groups, the city's ambition for inclusion is spelled out in 2016's Paris Efforts for integration of Parisian immigrants, human rights, fight against discrimination and woman and men equality. This document is organised in orientations, objectives and actions and had a budget of EUR 35.5 million in 2017 (Mairie de Paris, 2017). With regard to integration (with a budget of EUR 28.4 million in 2016) the city has three priorities: (1) promoting citizenship and equal access to rights and services; (2) integration and fighting exclusion by strengthening solidarity mechanisms for the most vulnerable Parisians of migrant origin (e.g. social action, employment, health, language learning);(3) promoting the countries of origin, cultures and heritage of those migrants who have contributed to shaping Paris' identity (Mairie de Paris, 2016). These integration objectives and their respective budgets have been formulated since 2005 and the budget increased by four times, from EUR 6.7 million in 2005 to more than EUR 28 million in 2016, reflecting the city's commitment to this policy. These priorities are implemented not only through the specific action funded by this policy across different departments but also through generic actions that address all publics (Mairie de Paris, 2016).

In addition, the city reacted to the increased arrivals of refugees and asylum seekers in 2015 by developing a targeted approach: "Mobilisation of the community of Paris to welcome refugees". The refugee reception and subsequent integration strategy will be explained in Section 2.1.4.

Further, the city is relying on the City Policy's resources to improve service provision in the most exposed areas where the migrant population is often overrepresented[8]. Concentration and adaptation of investments in those districts should contribute to increasing the responsiveness of universal services and make them more appropriate to the specific needs of the population living in those areas.

Last, other policy tools indirectly tackle integration-related issues. In 2015, two strategic action plans were released in Paris aiming at decreasing inequalities among inhabitants. The "Parisian Pact to Fight Great Exclusion" was released in

2015 following the commitment to render the "fight against great exclusion" the main cause of the 2015-2020 municipal mandate. This plan was signed by the municipality along with the prefecture, the "*préfecture de police*" as well as partner public bodies (e.g. ARS, CAF) and non-governmental organisations (e.g. FNARS). It outlines the collective and coordinated effort to assist populations who are in situation of extreme poverty and living on the street. Several points of the plan outline actions that either indirectly or specifically concern the integration of migrants. Likewise, the 'Parisian Pact for Insertion through work' sets the city's objectives by 2020 for favouring access to the labour market. This plan acknowledges migrant specificities when accessing the labour market such as the language barrier.

Key actors for the implementation of policies for integration and inclusion at the local level

As explained above the city (*ville de Paris*) is both a municipality and a department. At the political level, the Council of Paris, and the mayor elected by the council, hold a dual role by presiding over both the city and the department, which remain distinct entities, and holding both responsibilities. Along with the mayor, 27 elected vice-mayors supervise specific policy areas.

The General Secretariat of the City of Paris coordinates the actions of Directorates: public function units which support the functioning of the council and implement the policies. The General Secretariat is the main contact point of the different vice-mayors but directorates are also in direct contact with them. Directorates are responsible for municipal and departmental competences at the administrative level (for a visual representation, see Figure 2.2 above). There is no automatic correspondence between directorates and vice-mayors (i.e. a directorate can correspond to several vice-mayors and a vice-mayor can be responsible for topics managed by different directorates).

There is no specific department in charge of migrant integration; however, several vice-mayors participate in functional migrant integration and in the city's efforts regarding migrant and refugee integration.

1. The Vice-Mayor in charge of Solidarity, the fight against exclusion, child protection and refugee reception has been managing the response to refugee integration and oversees 30% of the city's budget and the social assistance centres (CASVP). This Deputy Mayor supervises the "Mobilisation of the Community of Paris for refugees" plan, which requires the participation of 9 other Vice-mayors.
2. The Vice-Mayor in charge of Security, Prevention, City Policy and integration oversees all questions related to integration and the implementation of City Policy at the local level
3. The Vice-Mayor in charge of Equality, between women and men, fight anti-discrimination and human rights.
4. The Vice-Mayor of local democracy, participation, associations, youth and employment oversees matters related to access to employment (e.g. Plan to access employment, language learning for refugees and asylum seekers, Mission locale de Paris) (see 2.4).

5. The Vice-Mayor in charge of the social and solidary economy, social innovation and the circular economy focuses on economic integration (e.g. entrepreneurship programmes for refugees) (See 2.4).

In terms of the provision of universal services, immigrants are among the beneficiaries of the services provided by the city across its directorates and services. Under the supervision of the General Secretariat (see 2.1.1) some Directorates are key players in implementing policies for migrant integration:

- Directorate of Democracy, Citizens and Territories (DDCT) manages access to rights, opportunities and the fight against discrimination. This directorate coordinates actions that are indicated within the budget document for "Paris efforts for integration of Parisian immigrants, human rights, fight against discrimination and women and men equality" (see section 2.1.3). In particular the service for Equality, Integration and Inclusion (SEII) is dedicated to migrant integration, anti-discrimination, human rights and equality between man and women.
- The Centre for Social Action of Paris (CASVP) which provides social services through the 20 centres in the city (delivers social allowances, implements social services for vulnerable residents, organises workshops, etc.).
- The *Délégation à la politique de la ville et à l'intégration* (DPVI) is the focal point for the implementation of the City Policy in close coordination with the Directorate of Urbanism (DU) for urban renewal and urban planning purposes.
- DASCO – Directorate of School Affairs
- DAE - Directorate of 'Attractivity' and Employment
- DLH -Directorate for Housing and Habitat
- DASES- Directorate of Social Action for Children and Health

Moreover, associations and NGOs undertake a substantive share of the services provided to vulnerable groups in Paris and migrants in particular (see 2.3.2 on interaction with non-state actors). For instance, over 40 associations are implementing first reception actions towards migrants and refugees and countless others are involved in integration activities in Paris[9].

Seek integration policy coherence at local level

The city ambition to integrate migrants is clear: it translates in an every-year increasing budget to cover these efforts and in a clear communication from the Mayor who defines Paris as "a global city of immigration and mixing of cultures". However more could be done in terms of seeking policy coherence and avoid horizontal fragmentation of policy-making and service delivery. Despite the high number of municipal directorates and policies (i.e. City policy, pact for exclusion, pact for insertion) which have a direct impact on integration, there is no working group to align the objectives and measuring the results that collectively the city is achieving in this area. As it emerges also from interviews with municipal operational services who deal with integration (see Section 2.4.3) the city vision does not necessarily translate in implementation guidelines. On the contrary the response of the city to receive and integrate asylum seekers and refugees adopted in September 2015, on the wake of a massive solidarity demonstrations from civil society, translated into 18 actionable steps and a governance mechanism involving nine municipal directorates.

The municipality sets aside dedicated resources and highlights an explicit ambition in terms of migrant integration: this already place Paris very high in benchmarking with other European cities analysed in this study. The remaining steps to improve integration governance, at horizontal level and across levels of government, comprise of different components. Here are suggested some tools, based on the findings of the Checklist (OECD, 2018) and the indicators of the INTI-CITIES framework (INTI-CITIES, 2009):

- Administrative cooperation: develop a strategic plan based on the city's ambition and vision. Integrate the plan into relevant policy portfolios and set milestones and delivery standards that every administration engages to achieve. A good example of administrative cooperation across departments for integration issues is the city of Vienna;
- Working partnerships: the municipality adopts a strategy for liaising with NGOs and private partners with regards to migrant integration. This can be done in terms of co-ordination mechanisms, clearing the goals and role of partner organisations also through contracts and formal agreements. Paris experimented new practices with partner organisations since September 2015 and the creation of the Platform for addressing refugee integration (see Section 2.1.4). An engagement chart with civil society has been elaborated in Glasgow and sectoral platforms involving NGOs on migrant integration issues have been experimented in Barcelona (see 2.3.2);
- Governance: set up a permanent inter-departmental committee for migrant integration involving the directorates that contribute directly to the budget "Paris Efforts for integration of Parisian immigrants, human rights, fight against discrimination and woman and men equality" along the lines of the platform established in September 2015 to align several departments around the 18 engagements for refugees. In addition, the municipality could appoint an "Integration Agent" or unit which would lead the interdepartmental committee and report directly to the cabinet of the mayor. In this sense, the cities of Gothenburg and Athens can offer valuable experience; and
- Evaluation: regularly collect data on the achievements of city's migrant integration policies and report results to the public. Paris could invest in putting indicators in place that measure success and failure in integration has it is analysed in Section 2.3.3.

Communication on migrant integration

In response to the perception of migration among the public opinion (see 1.2) and to improve general understanding of local actions towards migrant, the municipality is trying to highlight the positive contributions of inter-cultural activities and diversity to the city. Some initiatives seek to produce data on migrants' positive contributions. For instance, the city measured business creation by foreigners (see project APUR described in Objective 8). In the past, the city promoted a communication campaign to improve citizens' perception of most exposed neighbourhoods as detailed in 2.2.2. The municipality organised extraordinary public sessions, to which NGOs were also invited, to inform longstanding communities of new policies and programmes regarding asylum seekers and migrants. However, further communication with citizens about migration data and municipal policies to integrate migrant populations remains essential.

2.1.3. Objective 3: Ensure access to, and effective use of financial resources that are adapted to local responsibilities for migrant integration

The Parisian budget comprises its own resources and funds transferred by the central government. The 2017 operating expenditure was EUR 7 864 million and operating income EUR 8 358 million. Its investment spending was EUR 1 687 million and revenue EUR 605 million. In terms of investments Paris spent the highest share (43%) on Planning, urban services and environment; followed by investments in housing (17%) and general services (13%) (see Figure 2.3) (Mairie de Paris, 2017).

Figure 2.3. Expenditures by policy in the 2017 Parisian projected budget

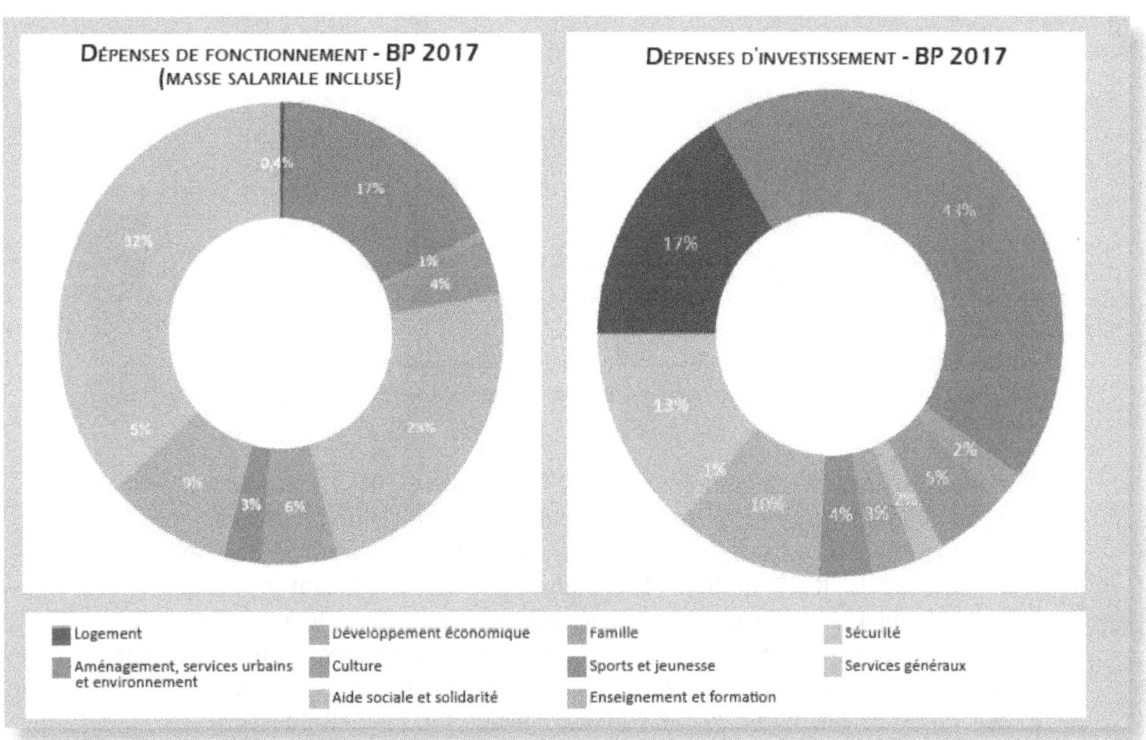

Source: Paris (2017), Expenditures by public policy in the projected budget 2017.

As mentioned before (see Figure 2.2), the Municipality has devoted a budget to migrant integration since 2006 (Mairie de Paris, 2016). This document includes both the expenditures for specific actions to adapt universal services to migrant needs and it keeps record of the costs of universal municipal services that were delivered to migrant beneficiaries. For instance, the amount of City Policy subsidies allocated to NGOs are reflected in the budget for migrant integration proportionally to the size of the migrant popoulation in the neighbourhood benefitting from those policies (i.e. 28.8% of residents in XYZ neighborhood).

According to this document, expenditure for migrant integration in Paris is estimated at EUR 28 million in 2016, a 25.7% increase from 2015, out of the total operational budget for both Paris Municipality and Department (Mairie de Paris, 2017).

Figure 2.4. Paris' integration budget by priority areas

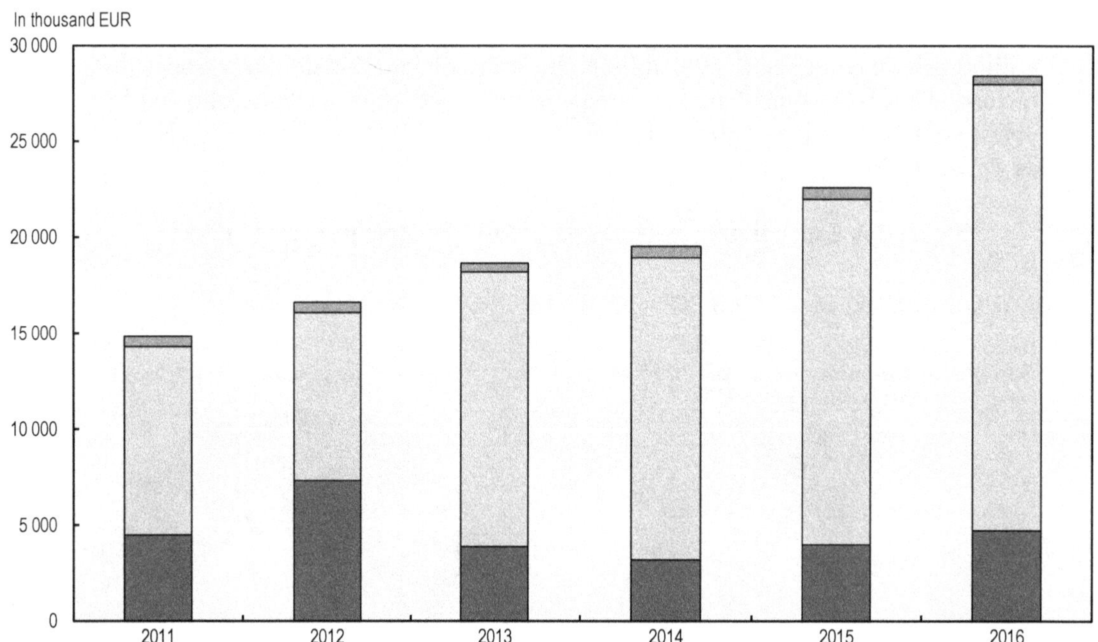

Source: « Communication sur l'effort de la collectivité parisienne en faveur de l'intégration des Parisiens immigrés, pour les droits humains, la lutte contre les discriminations et l'égalité femmes-hommes ».

The plan to support integration (EUR 28.4 million in 2017) represents a cross-sectoral funding mechanism as it distributes/takes stock of all relevant credits across the city's directorates. In particular, the CASVP[10] received nearly half of the budget or EUR 13 million. The budget to support integration is part of a broader budget for equality between women and men, human rights and discrimination which in 2017 represented EUR 35.5 million in total. Another EUR 5 million were spent in 2017 for the plan supporting fight against severe exclusion (Mairie de Paris, 2017), which contributes to integration issues.

Further, the city also used the private sector for innovative funding solutions. For instance, the municipality of Paris started an innovative partnership with the non-profit civic crowdfunding platform Co-city in September 2016. Co-city is an NGO that supports local civil society initiatives in the aim of improving urban inclusivity and sustainability. In 2017, one of the projects voted by most people targeted the exclusion of migrants and vulnerable people with EUR 500 000. Since 2016, Co-city works with the Paris' projected budget to facilitate the development of projects by Priority neighbourhood residents and further engage them to participate in the institutional budget[11].

2.1.4. Multi-level governance of asylum seekers and refugee reception and integration mechanism

A municipal strategy for refugee reception and integration: the 18-point plan entitled "Mobilisation of the community of Paris to welcome refugees"

In October 2015, the city adopted the 18-point plan called "Mobilisation of the community of Paris to welcome refugees". It is a new strategic approach to respond to early reception, and later integration, needs of the refugees arrived from 2015 (Mairie de Paris, 2015b). The plan is coordinated by the Deputy Mayor in charge of Solidarity, fight against exclusion, child protection and refugee reception. Since the adoption of the plan, 25 000 persons have been sheltered. The 18 commitments of the plan are applied to actions and streamlined in the city budgets for social policy.

The first block of engagements of the city aims at fulfilling Paris' responsibilities as a city and a department in terms of protection of vulnerable groups (i.e unaccompanied minors, alone woman with children and pregnant, etc.), social follow up in public space, access to rights comprised in Paris responsibilities. In this sense, in 2016, a specific entity - DEMIE (*Dispositif d'évaluation des mineurs isolés étrangers*) - was established in partnership with the Red Cross to evaluate the situation of unaccompanied minors, and the municipality reinforced the shelter units for this group. Further, specific needs of pregnant women and women with children are addressed through specific accommodation facilities (see Box 2.3).

The second block aims at improving asylum-seeker reception and refugee integration in the city of Paris. While providing shelter for asylum seekers is not a municipal competence (see paragraph below on Asylum process step by step), the municipality of Paris, after discussions with NGOs and central authorities, created additional temporary accommodation facilities to respond to the formation of makeshift camps in the city: the First Welcome Centres (CPA) of Porte de la Chappelle and Ivry (see Box 2.3). In addition, the municipality increased local integration efforts by improving access to health. Expand the offer of language courses by funding associations that give language courses to asylum seekers without access to OFII courses and by complementing the OFII courses. It equally supported integration measures for accessing employment and entrepreneurship (e.g. public employment agents in shelters, and support NGOs that enhance migrant entrepreneurship).

The third block of commitments aims at improving the collaboration with partner organisations and support civil society solidarity towards asylum seekers. An "external" platform including non-state stakeholders (associations, NGOs, etc.) meets twice a year to monitor the implementation of the plan and has been involved in the formulation of a holistic municipal Integration Plan for refugees that was developed in 2017.

Last, the remaining commitments aim at enhancing Paris' international position as a defender of human rights and solidarity.

The plan is carried out by municipal services as well as deconcentrated national agencies such as *Pôle Emploi* (the French public employment service), the welfare office (CAF), and NGOs. An "internal" coordination platform was created in the municipality, under the responsibility of the Deputy Mayor aiming at ensuring the consistency of refugee initiatives across the different departments (School affairs, City Policy, Housing and emergency accommodation, labour, etc.) of the General Secretariat. The work carried out by this platform is carried out in close coordination with the Prefecture.

Box 2.3. The First Reception Humanitarian Centres in Paris (*Centres Humanitaires de Premier Accueil*) in Porte de la Chapelle and Ivry

In 2016, the municipality of Paris spearheaded the development of two First Reception Humanitarian Centres (CPA) in Paris for recently arrived people in the city. The Mayor of Paris expressed her willingness to "no longer accept the humanitarian and health situation of makeshift camps developing in Paris". The financing of the CPA in Porte de la Chapelle (18th arrondissement, in the north of Paris) represents a successful co-financing mechanism between municipal and national levels (Ministry of Interior). The municipality initially reacted by investing (in 2015) in emergency facilities. The initial investment for the CPA of La Chapelle is capped at EUR 8.1 million, financed by 80% with municipal budget and it progressively received national funding up to 20%. Further, the operational budget was also co-financed with 85% by the State and the rest by the municipality. Whereas 100% of the accommodation and health care facilities are funded by the State, the reception and orientation on site as well as the transportation (EUR 5 million budget), were partly financed (half) by each level of government. For the centre of Ivry, a neighbouring municipality in the south of Paris, the initial investment of EUR 11 million was also shared between the municipality (60%) and the State (40%) and the annual operating cost is capped at EUR 3.5 million (90% the state and 10% the City of Paris).

1. The first one is the CPA at Porte de la Chapelle, a transition shelter in the 18th Arrondissement, an area where migrants had previously gathered in street camps. Thanks to the multi-stakeholder presences the services provided include shelter for up to 10 days (in principle) and health support as well as initial administrative procedures. The NGO Emmaus Solidarité manages the centre and Médecins du Monde/Secours Catholique provides health services including counselling and psychological support. The national agency OFII (responsible for integration measures and administrative proceedings for immigration), is represented in the centre to provide an initial evaluation of the person's administrative situation. The specific administrative needs of unaccompanied minors are addressed by the departmental organism dedicated to them (DEMIE). The local authority set up a

multi-stakeholder steering committee (*Comité de pilotage Porte de la Chapelle,* COPIL) meeting every week, involving NGOs. national agencies responsible for asylum (OFII), the Regional Prefecture and the Prefecture de Police representing the national government allowing to offer shelter and health care while registering in the national asylum system. The La Chapelle humanitarian centre closed on 31 March 2018 as per the initial engagement. Between 11 November 2016 and 31 March 2018, 18 980 single men received temporary shelter at the CPA in Porte de la Chapelle (450 beds for single men in this facility).

2. The second one, is the Ivry CPA for isolated women, families and vulnerable migrants, which opened in 2017 on land owned by the Paris municipality in the neighbouring city of Ivry thanks to close collaboration between both local authorities. In this centre, which has a maximum capacity of 400 people (families with children and women alone), the services provided are the same (initial administrative procedure, shelter and health support) yet the length of stay is longer since they can be sheltered for 3 months. The medical team integrated in the complex offers regular consultation tailored to the specificities of the public through the presence of the associations Paediatrics of the World and Gynaecologist without borders. Between 15 February 2017 and 11 April 2018, 2 334 people including 868 children were hosted in this facility.

If appropriate to their administrative situation, the objective of these shelters is to provide a temporary place to live before entering in the national reception system (i.e. CADA, etc., see 2.1.4, 2.4.4.Annex C). However out of the 66 704 persons welcomed in the centre, only 15 600 were then rehoused in appropriate structures within the national scheme. This is due to the difficulties of the national system to find appropriate accommodation across the country and relieve the structures in Île-de-France and Paris in particular where 40% of the regional reception shelters are located. Due to the congestion in the national system, Paris' efforts to provide emergency shelter to newcomers remain insufficient to cover the demand. In March 2018, France Terre d'Asile Maraude found that 1 885 migrants were living in makeshift camps.

Source: Authors' elaboration.

Further, in June 2017, the Mayor of Paris suggested in a letter to the Ministry of Interior a national plan to better take care of humanitarian migrants in France stressing the need to better protect unaccompanied minors, increase national distribution of asylum seekers and deepen refugee integration.

The asylum process step by step in 2018

In 2015, an asylum reform changed the asylum application process aiming at simplifying and speeding up the asylum procedure. As mentioned above, since the increased arrivals of asylum seekers in 2015, the system is bulking, and the delays for registration and assessment are still long, which drives some applicants into homelessness. It is essential to grasp the local impacts of asylum legislation and procedures. This is, for instance the case for Paris given the fact that the region is an asylum hub and highly attractive for migrants by its international reputation, metropolitan labour pool and previous migrant cohorts (see 1.1). The new legislation proposed in February 2018 attempts at reducing the delay of assessment by shortening it from the current average of 14 months on average to 6 months.

The asylum procedure is a national competence and local authorities are not involved in the process. Once registered as asylum seekers in France at the "single desk" uniting Prefecture and OFII services and before the OFPRA decision on their status, through the DNA, *Dispostif national daAsile* (National Asylum system) managed by the OFII, asylum seekers are entitled to stay in the national territory and to receive a specific financial allowance: the *"Allocation pour demandeur d'asile"* or ADA, which is financed by the national government and distributed monthly by the OFII[12]. Along with the financial support, asylum seekers have access to universal health (PUMA), childhood education and temporary accommodation assigned by the OFII within the *Dispositf national d'accueil* (DNA). NGOs play a crucial role in the DNA by managing temporary accommodation structures. Local authorities are not involved in the decision to open temporary accommodation for asylum seekers within the DNA, which is a decision made by the prefectures. Theoretically, asylum seekers are entitled to accommodation yet the existing capacities are limited. In France, asylum seekers are not allowed to work (except if after nine months their asylum request has not been handled) or receive government language courses. A current law is under discussion at the moment of publication at the national level which might change the rights of asylum seekers.

Since the 2015 reform, the process to access the DNA is made up of five key steps (see 2.4.4.Annex C).

The mechanism for dispersing and sheltering asylum seekers

Although there is no dispersal mechanism that allocates an obligatory quota of asylum seekers to every municipality, since 2015 and the call of the State for volunteer municipalities, there has been a strong political will to create new places in the DNA and to equally distribute the structures within the national territory at the department level. Distributing and sheltering asylum seekers is a policy domain managed in coordination between national bodies (i.e. Ministry of Interior, Prefectures and OFII) and partner NGOs, in which local authorities do not participate. The Asylum Department (within the Interior Ministry, DGEF) is in charge of designing and piloting solutions to enlarge the asylum system. This department publishes calls for proposals to create new reception facilities. These calls for proposals take into consideration the number of asylum seekers that are already hosted in each region. The calls are elaborated in line with the regional reception plan (*Schéma regional d'accueil des demandeurs d'asile et refugiés,* SRADAR) prepared by the prefectures. The document aims at improving the equitable distribution of temporary housing facilities across the region, ensure information flows with local authorities and improve the fluidity of the asylum procedure and coordination between territorial satellites of national bodies (Prefecture-OFII) (Ministère de l'Intérieur, 2016a). Initially the SRADAR was only addressed to support prefects in accompanying asylum seekers and it has recently been extended to refugees. The calls are then published by the prefectures and associations can respond to them. Thus, local authorities do not participate or are consulted directly in the selection process of opening accommodation facilities for the DNA and their location and management is regulated through a contract between regional prefects and the NGO. In addition to the DNA, in 2015 the State called for volunteer municipalities, to offer long term housing for refugees and 1600 places had been offered until December 2017. Accommodation facilities are financed under the national budget BOB 303 for social action. In *Île-de France*, the Migrant plan represents 10% of the total budget for social action that is managed by the Asylum Department through prefects.

The OFII centralises the information about where spots are available in DNA facilities across the country from the NGOs managing the centres. 70% of the spot are allocated by the territorial offices (alongside the prefectures) to the asylum seekers who applied locally at the OFII. The remaining 30% are allocated by the central OFII and are reserved to the most vulnerable asylum seekers.

The accommodation system for asylum seekers in France is complex and composed of multiple forms of facilities according to the administrative status of the beneficiary[13]. There are three main types of temporary accommodation for asylum seekers connected to the DNA in which the OFII can find available shelter for vulnerable asylum seekers: CADA (the main type of shelter facilities with extensive social and administrative support), HUDA (emergency facilities) and AT-SA (emergency facilities) (see Table 2.1). A concern after 2015 has been the lack of accommodation facilities to face the existing needs of asylum seekers. In 2016, there were 50 000 places in accommodation facilities for asylum seekers in France, whereas the OFPRA registered 87 000 asylum petitions. Since 2015, the Asylum Department has increased the number of places available and there are currently 80 000 places for accommodation for asylum seekers. The 2018 asylum law aims at creating 7 500 new places in 2018-2019 for accommodation facilities of asylum seekers. In Paris, in March 2017, 3 907 asylum seekers were hosted in AT-SA, CADA and HUDA facilities (see 2.4.4.Annex C).

Table 2.1. Number of asylum seekers hosted in Paris in March 2017, per reception type

COMMUNE	AT-SA	CADA	HUDA	TOTAL
Paris	94	645	3 168	3 907

Source: OECD (Forthcoming), *The Location of Asylum Seekers in OECD Regions and Cities*.

Further, since 2015, along with the traditional structures of reception and accommodation of asylum seekers, new transitory shelter categories were created by the national level in the context of camp dismantling to cover the period between homelessness and accessing the DNA for asylum seekers (i.e. CAO in France –usually created by Prefects with mayor approval-, CHUM in the case of Île-de-France region). In the case of Paris as mentioned above, the temporary humanitarian centres (CPA) were created (see Box 2.3). Last, the *Centre d'hébergement d'urgence* CHUs (Emergency Shelter Centres), which are technically outside the asylum system have played a critical role in hosting asylum seekers and refugees that were evacuated by the prefecture (in the first months of 2017 9 100 a priori asylum seekers were place by the prefecture in CHU). There are 100 CHU in the Île-de France. These are temporary social shelters, based on French social rights law, that all person can access regardless of their status (unconditional principle) in theory for how long is needed to find a sustainable housing solution. In Paris these structures are managed by different public (CASVP) and non-public actors (Emmaus solidarité, etc.). Once their application is filled, asylum seekers should be transferred from CHU to CADA which usually should take up to two months (OECD interviews with Paris Prefecture).

Governmental support for refugees

As mentioned, there is no obligation to house or provide other specific support to recognised refugees in the French system (see 2.4.2). However, in interviews with the OECD, and how it is stated in the Inter-ministerial Integration Committee (ICC) (see Section 2.1.1) in June 2018 (Comité interministériel á l'intégration, 2018[2]), French authorities express their willingness to support this group due to its specific characteristics (i.e. the lack of family and community network, language skills and financial means, etc.) that increase their obstacles in accessing housing solutions. The committee announces a shift: from January 2019 refugees will benefit, during the first months after recognition, from personalised accompany measures to facilitate their access to health care, social services, language courses and professional training. In addition to expanding specific measures for refugees' access to labour market (see Section 2.4.1) the Committee announced that by 2020 the holistic models for refugees integration piloted by NGOs will be extended to all regions. This include expanding projects such as Reloref[14] implemented by France Terre d'Asile which combined housing of refugees issued from the DNA as well as developing networks and information tools for key actors involved in refugee integration such as housing and employment actors. In particular this project developed tools for supporting all actors accompanying refugees towards autonomy such as quick language assessment tool, guide for refugees' access to accommodation, training toolkit on refugee access to accommodation, etc.

One solution for refugees are the Temporary Accommodation Centers - CPH (*Centres provisoires d'hébergement*) - piloted since 2016 by the Asylum Department (Ministry of Interior). These facilities work like CADA but for recognised refugees. In 2017, 2 200 places were available in these facilities in France and the government aims at expanding CPH capacity to 5 000 spots by 2019. These facilities are attributed to NGOs through calls for proposal and local authorities are very marginally involved in the management of these structures present in their territories. Another mechanism for long-term refugee housing is the DIHAL platform described in Section 2.4.2.

Further, the ADA (economic allowance for asylum seekers) is allocated to refugees until the month after the decision on asylum status has been announced. From the moment they are recognised, refugees have access to minimum income allowance (RSA)[15] as all other citizens with insufficient means (see Section 2.4.3). Administrative delays in the provision of RSA[16] mean refugees encounter periods during which they have absolutely no revenue, which hampers the integration process (especially as they are not allowed to work during the asylum period or learn the language through government courses).

In general Paris social services noticed, as is the case in other cities analysed in this study, that the passage from asylum seekers to refugees can be problematic and many status holders rely on municipal social services and shelters. According to OECD interviews conducted with the CASVP, the national strategy that stops at the moment of recognition is not sufficiently linked to local policies for integration. While they noticed that since 70 % of users of social assistance points (PSA) are recognised refugees (see Section 2.4.3) most of them were not hosted in CADA. In fact, those hosted in these structures usually receive the necessary support to find a sustainable housing solution.

Cross-sectoral governance mechanism for asylum seeker and refugee integration

Since the asylum reform in 2015 efforts have been put in place to better coordinate the local with the national level with regard to the dispersal mechanism for asylum seekers. The SRADA plan developed by the regional level, described above, is an example of these efforts. Moving beyond the reception horizon, in 2018 the French government focused its efforts on strengthening integration mechanisms for refugees, considering the multidimensional and multi-level character of their settling in process.

To strengthen coherence across policies relevant for refugee integration, in January 2018, the government appointed an Inter-ministerial delegate for refugee integration, embedded within the Ministry of Interior. With an overall mandate for coordinating inter-ministerial policies on this matter the delegate will be overseeing the implementation of the recent National Strategy for Refugee Integration (2018-2020). This strategy was developed by the Asylum Department of the Interior Ministry (General Directorate for Foreigners in France - DGEF) based on a stock-take of refugee integration in France conducted in 2017 through a participatory process. Five sectoral work groups – composed of ministries, non-governmental organisations, sectoral start-ups and experts – contributed in analysing the current situation and identifying the priorities for action around the following five subjects: (1) access to rights, (2) access to housing, (3) access to employment, to professional training and language learning, (4) access to the health system and (5) access to culture, sports and social activities. Following this workgroups, the Association of French Departments (ADF) was also consulted. The Action Plan gathered sixty actions across the five sectors and a cross governance section to ensure that refugee integration processes are coordinated and comprehensive.

Some measures of the Plan, whose implementation is foreseen in three years, are starting to be developed whereas other measures are still being discussed. The budget that each ministry will allocate for implementing the measures, will fall within their competences. Reflections are still ongoing about the indicators for monitoring the action Plan.

In terms of governance, the Plan has considered the creation of three coordination instances: (1) An inter-services committee at the national level meeting every two months to ensure information-sharing between the refugee integration focal points of each ministry; (2) local steering committees will be organised by the prefects and include associations, deconcentrated services and agencies of the state, local authorities, businesses and NGOs; (3) Last, an annual national conference in which integration actors will be invited along with State services to co-ordinate NGOs on refugee integration policies in France.

The strategic plan foresees especially concrete actions to improve refugees' access to housing, health, language learning and employment, as well as the establishment of an integration path based on individualised support that is adapted to the personal vulnerabilities in the first months after status acquisition.

2.2. Block 2: Time and space keys for migrants and host community to live together

This section aims at describing the leading principles along which reception and integration policies are designed at city level. Across the cities analysed in the study sample, the concepts of time and proximity appear to be essential in imagining durable integration solutions. Time refers to the life-long process of establishing oneself in a city, and the continuum of solutions that have to be provided from day one and along this process. Besides the objective of facilitating and hastening the integration of newcomers, cities must offer entry points for foreign-born or native-born individuals with a migrant background, to facilitate the different aspects of their well-being and development throughout their lives. Space is understood as proximity and is well illustrated by the concept of *Connecting* that many cities have adopted in their approach to integration. This concept acknowledges that inclusion does not result automatically from living in the same city or street, it requires sustained interaction. Cities have a role to play in encouraging such interaction, by supporting local level initiatives and creating public spaces, where connections among different groups can spark a dialogue among all components of the society.

2.2.1. Objective 4: Design integration policies that take time into account through migrants' lifetimes and status evolution

It is increasingly evident that migrant integration requires public action over time. The Paris administration has acknowledged the concept of time is crucial in its action plan "Mobilisation of the Paris community for refugee reception" (2015b): the "emergency response is inseparable from the preparation of future integration." The municipality outlines that "language learning, access to culture, employment and housing are equally essential conditions for integration" and that "emergency reception in decent conditions and refugee integration are not two different steps which would come one after the other" but rather complementary elements to promote favourable integration. This time principle along with the ones of (1) equal treatment and (2) municipal and civil society mobilisation have been incorporated into the municipal budget since 2016.

Such awareness that integration should begin from day one is not dissociated from the need to provide support to migrants and refugees during the long process of integration.

Ensuring migrant and refugee access to rights over time

The first priority area of Paris integration strategy is "Citizenship, Equality and Access to Rights" ("*Citoyenneté, égalité et accés aux droits*") aiming at eliminating obstacles to citizenship, legality, and access to legal and social rights.

This is done by offering targeted legal assistance and making sure mainstream services, in particular social ones, are adapted to migrant characteristics. The objective is guaranteeing that over time migrants can access universal services autonomously.

Migrants and refugees' access to rights is first of all subject to the regularisation of their status. In France, as in many other countries, administrative delays[17] can lead to uncertainty and long waiting times for receiving legal permits. In the meantime, regular status is attested to by the delivery of several *récépissés (receipts)* which last three or six months. These *récépissés* temporarily provide proof of residence, substituting for the residence permits, and grant rights to access welfare allowances, the labour market, social housing or professional training. It has recently been noted that delays in renewing these *récépissés* make access to rights difficult and might break the path towards migrant integration (Taché, 2018).

The city has invested in several mechanisms for facilitating migrants in accessing their residence permits. Under the Direction of Juridical Affairs several free consultation services are offered, in partnership with the bar of Parisian lawyers, across every district's town hall. Other specific initiatives (i.e. *Relais d'accès au droit* - RAD, *Points d'accès au droit*, *Maison de justice et du droit*, etc.) offer legal consultation to all the population with a specific focus on foreigners who represent over 50% of their public (Mairie de Paris, 2016).

The translation of administrative documents and interpreting services are valuable steps to ensure equal access to public services at different steps of a migrant's life. The Centre for social action (CASVP) assures that their services are available in different languages by recruiting translators and translating administrative procedures for medical, social and school support services (i.e. the *Dispositif parisien de réussite éducative* offers translation services to schools within the priority areas of the City Policy). In addition, every year a guide is produced by the municipality for non-French speaking Parisians "Vivre à Paris" in English, Spanish and Arabic compiling information about the services offered by the city in terms of employment, housing, reception, health, etc.

Another valuable entry point for all vulnerable groups in ensuring their access to rights and services are the five PIMMS (*Points d'information et de médiation multiservices*) - Multi service Information and Mediation Points). These 'anti-exclusion points' aim at ensuring that most vulnerable groups living in disadvantaged neighbourhoods can access services by offering personalised assistance with bureaucratic procedures and adapted information. These are not parallel services but entry points to guide vulnerable residents through universal services. The service is also mobile with a bus "*Mairie mobile*" visiting three sites per week in disadvantaged neighbourhoods. The city estimates that 24.5% of PIMMS visitors have a migration background (foreigners and immigrant population), they account for 30% in the neighbourhoods targeted by the City Policy (Mairie de Paris, 2016).

2.2.2. Objective 5: Create spaces where interaction between migrant and native-born communities enable both groups to move physically and socially closer

The integration process is one of mutual adaptation and concerns both migrants and natives. Finding opportunities to bridge the divide between migrants and Parisians is a key concern that the municipality addresses along with other government levels and with civil society organisations.

Implement inclusive urban policies to de-segregate the migrant population

One strategy is to strengthen cultural, education and mobility services in those neighbourhoods where migrants concentrate. As described the City Policy is the main tool in this direction (see Box 2.2).

Further efforts strive to make disadvantaged areas more attractive for Parisians who live in less diverse neighbourhoods. In this sense, and to reduce misconceptions about areas mainly in the northeast being "don't-go-zones", Paris developed a campaign renaming them "Must-go-zones" to attract residents and improve their image.

Figure 2.5. The "Must-Go-Zones" municipal campaign to attract residents and tourists to disadvantaged areas

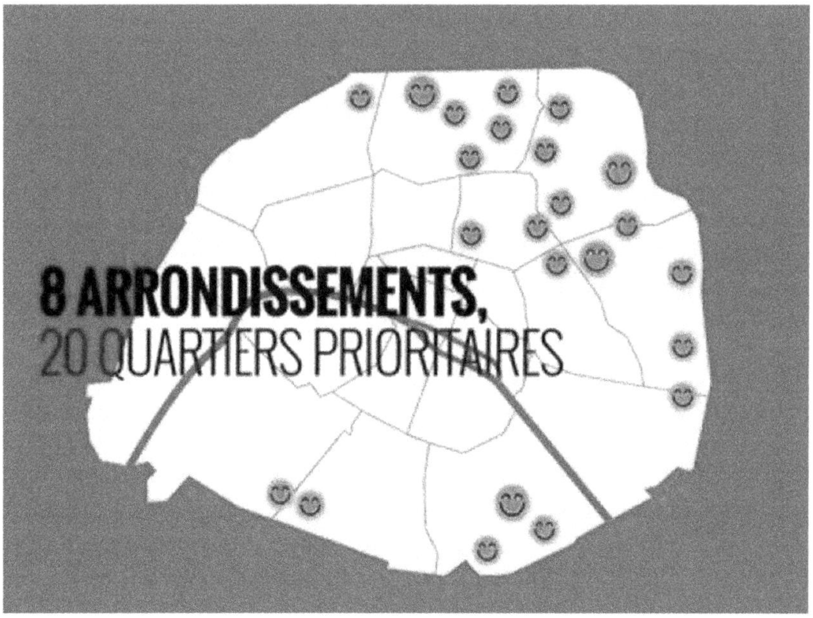

Source: City of Paris Campaign.

Another example is the creation of the 104[18], an artist platform for cultural production and diffusion for publics and artists from all over the world. The Municipality opened the 104 in 2007 in the 19th arrondissement, which is often stigmatised as being a peripheral area characterised by a strong presence of migrants. Over 39 000m^2 are available for all publics to cultivate their artistic talents (dance, yoga, music, etc.), to attend free classes and for associations to use as meeting places. There is also a stat-up incubator for experimentation, art and innovation. The 104 collaborates with local civic society initiatives in its surrounding area and is increasingly used by bottom-up projects linked to migrant integration. The artistic character of the 104 has been requested for language learning activities for recently arrived migrants through theatre classes allowing the interaction and cultural exchange between migrants and long-standing artists. The municipality partially funds an annual forum at the 104 to celebrate and promote - through shows, workshops and classes - the rich cultural diversity of northeast neighbourhoods and waves of migration that have taken place there throughout history.

Some municipal libraries have launched initiatives designed to bridge the geographical gap between libraries and shelters for migrants and refugees by providing their services inside the shelters and by inviting migrants to visit libraries. These collaborations enabled refugees to borrow books and make use of the libraries to access the Internet, allowing them to be linked with their families, and their countries through social media and the press.

Municipal initiatives to facilitate the connection between recently arrived migrants and native-born residents

In Paris, civil society organisations and NGOs have historically played an essential role in organising activities and offering key services for migrant integration in the city. Volunteer work is crucial in providing food aid, legal advice and social support among others (see 2.4). As observed in other cities analysed in this study, the 2015 peak in asylum seeker arrivals triggered a wave of solidarity from civil society and fostered innovative bottom-up initiatives. To facilitate the connection between existing initiatives and the wave of empathy from Parisian residents, the municipality launched in 2015, the web platform *"Je m'engage"* (In English: "I commit") to facilitate matching between supply and demand for volunteer work. Local NGOs and civil society initiatives post their needs of volunteers, and interested residents directly answer and apply according to their availabilities and the kind of activity they want to pursue. The nature of the volunteer work is diverse (e.g. food and clothes collection, legal advice, school support, etc.) and residents can select their option through a localisation criterion as the platform is provided with a map where the different activities are developed.[19]

In addition, in 2016, the municipality launched an innovative booklet containing all information available for refugee reception in Paris. The *Guide d'accueil des réfugiés* à Paris (Guide for the reception of refugees in Paris) it contains information in terms of asylum procedures, access to health and social services, daily needs (e.g. where to find food, water, clothes, access to Wi-Fi). This booklet is mainly addressed to Parisians wanting to help recently arrived asylum seekers (rather than to asylum seekers or refugees themselves because of the kind of information provided and because it is not translated), and also indicates tips and errors to avoid when wanting to help asylum seekers (i.e. directing them towards the wrong shelters).

Box 2.4. Supporting bottom-up initiatives fostering proximity among diverse residents

Proximity between newcomers and long-standing communities is essential for migrant integration. Paris has several examples of civil society initiatives which aim at connecting migrants and refugees with their neighbourhoods and new societies. The municipality supports their sustainability through municipal investments or providing free spaces. For instance, the "Neighbours" Fridays – *"les vendredis des voisins"*- is an initiative organised by district town halls to allow foreign Parisians to meet their neighbours and obtain information about life in the district.

An example of a space that fosters connectivity among different groups is "*Les grands voisins*" (The Big Neighbours in English) is the biggest temporary regularised occupation in Europe on the premises of the previous hospital Saint-Vincent de Paul. It turned into a local meeting point for Parisians and migrants alike, as well as a tourist attraction well known for its innovative approach. In 2016, the old hospital facilities were repurposed by NGOs and used as a shelter and reception space to host refugee and asylum seekers. Along with the emergency shelter and administrative consultancy for refugees, there is a temporary campsite, start-up offices, artist studios and shops as well as a bar and an event space that every weekend is used for concerts, workshops, cinemas, etc. Refugees run small activities selling food, drinks and other items. This space not only offers refugees access to the expertise of experienced associations but it also brings people together from different socio-economic and cultural background for spending their free time doing their favourite activities.

Source: Authors' elaboration.

2.3. Block 3: Capacity for policy formulation and implementation

2.3.1. Objective 6: Build capacity and diversity in civil service, particularly in the key services that receive migrants and newcomers

As described in 2.2.1, the municipality is engaged in eliminating administrative and language barriers that migrants might encounter when accessing public services. In addition, training is offered to municipal agents in several departments (e.g. DDCT, DAC, DASES, DPP, DHL) on how to receive individuals with a foreign background. Every year the municipality spends over EUR 63 000 in diversity training and more than 1 000 municipal officers have been trained since 2004. The training sessions aim to favour equality and combat discrimination. Ten sessions are taught around legal frameworks applying to foreign citizens, anti-racist legislation, cultural contribution of migration and presentation of five geographical areas and cultures where migrants come from (Mairie de Paris, 2016).

The 2015 "Mobilisation of the community of Paris for refugee reception" plan also envisaged training activities for municipal public servants and social workers to boost their knowledge about refugees and improve reception, information and social support delivered to refugees.

Since 2016, the city of Paris invested in training for municipal health professionals to address the specific health needs of migrants especially how to treat psycho-trauma cases. To do so, the municipality collaborated with non-governmental associations (the associations Primo Levi and Traces) which develop training for both socio-medical professionals, school doctors and school social assistants. The municipality is also training librarians to receive users from foreign cultures. Other training in migrant rights and inter-cultural issues were offered in the Centre of Planning of Family Education (*Centre de planification et d'éducation familiale)* (CPEF) and departmental reception services SDA. There is a general tendency of Paris social services to better understand how to respond to the needs of the environment where they operate. This is done for instance by interacting with migrant communities and associations present in the district to seek their point of you and to inform them about the services available. Paris libraries spearheaded by offering services attractive to different communities (OECD interviews with CASVP).

Furthermore, the city employed 40 young people in civic service to both (1) support refugees hosted in Parisian shelters through language learning and administrative procedures and (2) develop cultural and leisure activities in the emergency accommodations (Mairie de Paris, 2015b).

2.3.2. Objective 7: Strengthen co-operation with non-state stakeholders, including through transparent and effective contracts

Associations and civil society organisations have traditionally been very strong players in migrant integration in Paris (Safi, 2014). Parisian associations and representations of national and international ones are numerous and highly active, either autonomously or in partnership with the city in all steps of migrant and refugee reception and integration. They provide support in a variety of domains including legal and life orientation (i.e. APTM, Secours Catholique, Cimade), food aid and clothes distribution (e.g. Les Restos du Coeur, Croix Rouge), health support, language learning, etc. The characteristics, history and size of the associations and civil society organisations are highly diverse from small neighbourhood collectives to national well-established NGOs. It is worth noting the high number of platforms, online tools, innovative third sector enterprises that have emerged since 2015 to respond to refugee arrivals and have remained active ever since.

The coordination between these associations and different government levels can take different forms. For instance, the city used to update every year an index of the associations acting in the domain of migrant reception, information and integration. The online platform "*Qui accueille*"[18] gathers information on all shelter and counselling services for the most vulnerable population in the city of Paris by district and domain of activity. As described, with regard to asylum seekers and refugees coordination is ensured through a platform bringing together twice a year the municipality and the partner stakeholders involved in this domain. Yet, associations participating in the study called for further strengthening coordination mechanisms among NGOs and between them and the municipality. Civil society organisations expressed their wish to make coordination more effective in the implementation level. They often have to segment their action by public or by stage of the integration process in order to respond to call for proposals that are issued by different municipal departments for a very specific public. They also called for coordination platforms where all actors operating in a sector (e.g. language classes, etc.) could meet and divide the work by geographic area or type of public.

NGOs also suggest that more long-term and holistic funding for integration activities would allow them to be more sustainable and effective. The bulk of the city's immigration initiatives are taken through subsidising (directly and indirectly) local associations. The DDCT (*Direction de la démocratie, des citoyens et des territoires*) itself has granted EUR 770 000 in grants to NGOs for integration-related projects in 2016. Yet this funding tends to be allocated in small amounts to diverse projects and on an annual basis. Further, since 28.8% of the population of City Policy neighbourhoods are migrants, the municipality also calculates at pro rata of this percentage, that subsidies to NGOs financed for City Policy-related matters by the DDCT contribute to the migrant integration policy of the city with an amount of EUR 1 098 642 in 2016 (Mairie de Paris, 2016). NGOs indicated that the grants system could be improved. Often NGOs have to 'slice up' their offer of services by specific group or action to align with the criteria of a plethora of different small grants issues by the diverse city divisions, the department or the prefecture. A more coherent approach within the different divisions towards migrants would allow for simplifying the system of calls for project and apply for more consistent grants, over longer periods and for more flexible projects addressing migrant publics. The system for allocating management of asylum seekers' reception centres to large and well-established NGOs such as Emmaus, France terre d'asile, the CAFDA or the Red Cross is managed through prefectures and the Ministry of Interior as described in Sections 2.1.4 and 2.4.4.Annex C.

The municipality takes the decision beforehand about which service will be executed by its own operational branches (i.e. CASVP, etc.) and which will be outsourced through call for proposals. Equally the city operational branches can respond to the call for proposals published by the city, the department or national authorities. Some key low threshold municipal services addressing the most vulnerable groups are ensured by NGOs. For instance, the Municipal Spaces Solidarity Insertion (*Espaces Solidarité Insertion*) offering shower, access internet, clean clothes, etc. are managed by partner associations (e.g. Fondation de l'Armée du salut, Aurore, Emmaus, Secours catholique, etc.).

In some cases, the outsourcing of tasks to NGOs is defined with contracts between the municipality and NGOs which clearly define the delegation of tasks and the responsibilities assigned to the NGO. A good example was the tripartite agreement signed to manage the CPA of La Chapelle between the municipality and national government with the NGO Emmaus Solidarité in 2016 which established the responsibilities of each stakeholder.

2.3.3. Objective 8: Intensify the assessment of integration results for migrants and host communities and their use in policy design

Indicators to track migrant integration at the national level

In the national population census (managed by the National Institute for statistics, INSEE), data is collected by nationality but also country of birth and nationality of birth since 1999 following the three categories described in the definition section: Foreign, Immigrant and Migrant Descent. Available data from the moment the migrant acquires French nationality at the local level is limited to localisation, employment and housing at the Department level. French law forbids the recording of information about racial or ethnic origins as well as religious affiliation.

Different government levels are aware that they generally lack harmonised indicators to systematically follow the implementation of their policy for integration and use the results for evidence-based policy making. For instance, the new Inter-Sectoral National Strategy for Refugee Integration (See Section 2.1.4) explicitly mentions evaluation of the action plan as one of the priorities.

Some services are innovating their evaluation practices. For instance, the Platform for sheltering and access to housing (*Délégation interministérielle à l'hébergement et à l'accès au logement* – DIHAL, see Box 2.4) has developed an evaluation mechanism to track the results of the housing programme, which since 2015 has benefitted 5 700 refugees across the country, as described in Section 2.4.2. This evaluation followed the individual trajectories of 300 beneficiaries and used different methodologies including participatory assessment, surveys and field visits. Also, the Platform keeps track of all the 1 600 housing units mobilised since 2016 (localisation, type of unit, etc.).

Monitoring migrant integration at the local level

Monitoring migrant results at the local level is essential to design integration policies that suit local needs.

Paris breaks statistics down in two groups of users of its public services (foreign and national) and distinguishes the expenditure for these two groups. As mentioned the Mairie de Paris (DDCT) produces a yearly report called *"Communication on the effort of the Parisian authority in favour of Parisian migrant integration, for human rights, the fight against discrimination and women-men equality*". The budget addressed to migrant integration by each directorate of local authority is mentioned and municipal actions for migrant integration described. This wealth of information on migrants' use of public services could lead to time series comparing access and spending for this group with the evolution of their socio-economic outcomes. In addition, this quantitative information could be combined with user surveys to measure the adaptation of the services to the needs and expectations of their beneficiaries. In this sense, an example is the survey conducted by CASV among migrant communities to understand the reasons for the very low use of municipal retirement houses by these communities and to understand how they could better respond to their needs. An example on use of statistics for evidence-based decision-making is the city of Gothenburg, which has developed an evaluation mechanism at the city and district level on disparities and integration outcomes. In Barcelona, thanks to a local register administered by the local authority (*Padrón*), the municipality gathers annual information about foreign born, foreign nationalities, as well as irregular migrants, their demographic profile, territorial distribution within the city and qualification, and publishes an annual report improving local policy makers' capacities to better assess policy design.

Pairs (as a city and department) finances almost entirely the *Parisian Atelier of Urbanism (APUR).* This research institute maps population outcomes per geographical location (district, neighbourhood), topic and year. Within the APUR, seven observatories are thematically specialised to improve the tracking of the relevant statistics and evaluate the actions implemented. Some study groups follow integration-relevant results for instance the Observatory for City-Policy-neighbourhoods the Parisian Observatory for Insertion and an Observatory of Housing.

A further difficulty in the measurement of migrants is that some groups are difficult to capture in official statistics such as irregular migrants, rejected asylum seekers or "Dublinés", who registered their first asylum claim in a EU country different than France, which tend also to be vulnerable migrant groups particularly exposed to homelessness. To monitor the invisible Parisians and assess homelessness in Paris (among which foreigners are over-represented (Apur, 2011)), the Deputy Mayor in charge of the fight against exclusion organised the Solidarity Night in February 2018. 3 000 people were identified and information was collected about their experience in accessing social services and the contact number (115) to access emergency shelters in Paris, which is managed by Samu Social (see 2.4.2).

The municipality established a partnership with the *École des hautes études en sciences sociales* to support applied research in the social sciences that looks into the local aspects of migration in Paris. The partnership seeks to better assess migration paths, characteristics and needs in order to support effective policy making (Mairie de Paris, 2015b). The municipality commissioned research on citizen accommodation practices developed by civil society associations in Paris and Île-de-France to accommodate migrants. The city tries to assess other aspects of migrant's presence in the city. For instance, the municipality commissioned local research on business creation by foreign entrepreneurs to the APUR.

2.4. Block 4: Sectorial policies for migrant integration

2.4.1. Objective 9: Match migrant skills with economic and job opportunities

Why is it important?

Employment is an essential aspect of the integration process. It is not only migrants' primary source of income, but also contributes to their integration by supporting their access to adequate housing and facilitating their interaction with native-born residents.

In France, about one in ten people of working age is a migrant and the unemployment rate of migrants is twice that of native-born French people, amounting to 18.1% in 2015 (Ministère de l'Intérieur, 2016b). According to INSEE data, in 2015, the unemployment rate of non-EU foreign (25%) was two and a half times higher than that of French citizens (10%) (*INSEE Enquête Emploi*). Recent OECD research has shed light on gaps on migrant access to the labour market (OECD, 2017b). The employment rate of recently arrived migrants is 25 percentage points lower than that of native-born. Only one out of three foreigners living in France for less than five years of working age is working.

In Île-de-France region, Figure 2.6 shows that 18% of the migrant population was unemployed in 2014-2015, 5 percentage points more than the rate of unemployed natives. While the unemployment rate of migrant women is lower than that of migrant men by 3 percentage points in the region, the gender gap in employment rates remains larger for migrants than natives, with a negative difference of 11 percentage points between the employment rates of migrant women (57%) and migrant men in the region (68%).

Figure 2.6. Labour market outcomes of foreign-born relative to native born in the region of Île-de-France 2014-2015

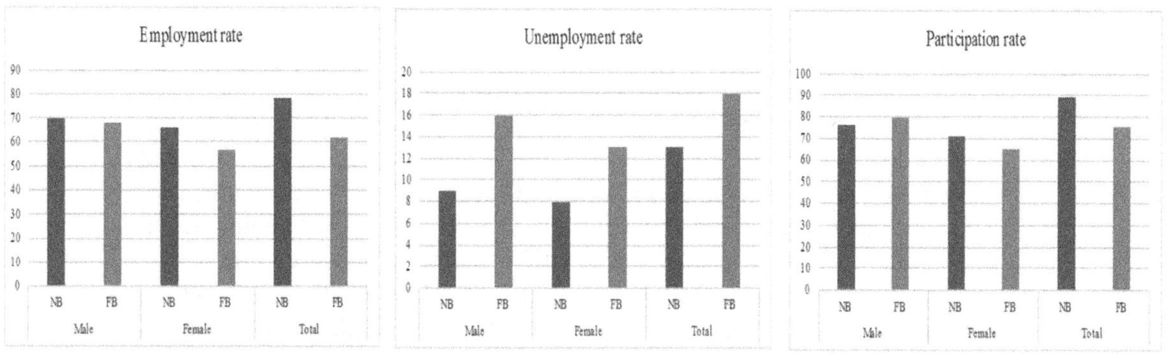

Note: "NB" refers to the "native-born population"; "FB" refers to the "foreign-born population".
Source: OECD database on migrant population outcomes at TL2 level.

In Île-de-France, highly-educated migrants struggle less than low-educated ones in finding a job (their unemployment rate is 5 percentage points lower than that of low-educated ones), but they struggle more relative to native born (see Figure 2.7). Highly-educated migrants show an employment shortfall of 11 percentage points relative to the highly-educated native-born population while the difference in employment rates between low-educated migrants and natives is 3 percentage points.

Figure 2.7. Labour market outcomes of foreign-born relative to native-born by level of education in Île-de-France, 2014-2015

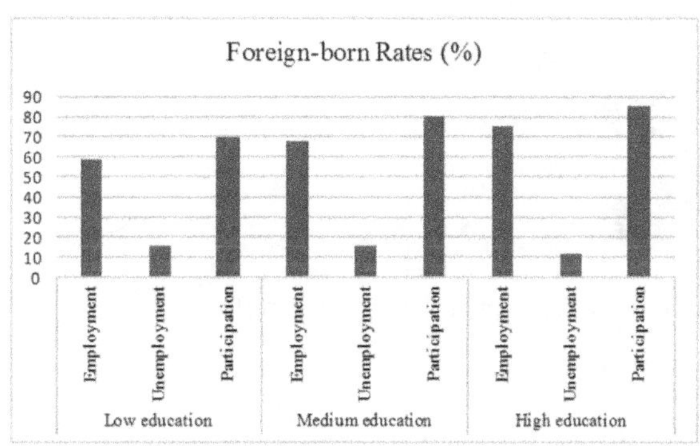

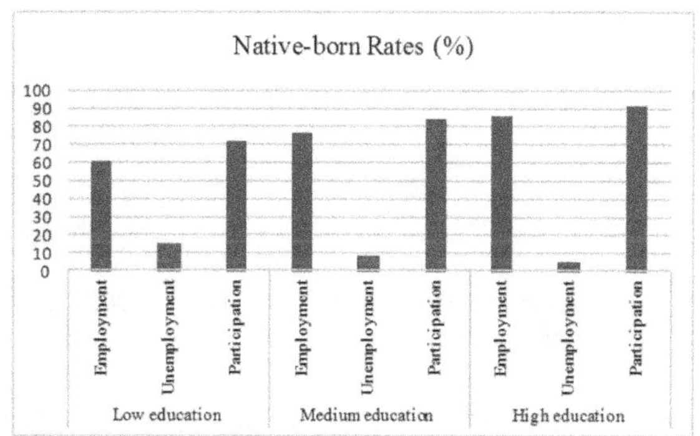

Note: Educational levels are based on ISCED 1997 ratings, from 0 to 6. A low-education level (0-2) reflects a primary education level, a medium -education level (34) corresponds to a secondary educational attainment and a high-education level (5-6) to a tertiary education level.
Source: OECD database on migrant population outcome at TL2 level.

While access to employment is a major aspect of economic integration, looking at the types of jobs migrants actually access provides a more comprehensive picture of migrants' participation in the labour market. More specifically, over-qualification is a recurring issue for migrants in France. In 2012-2013, more than a fourth of employed foreign-born individuals with a tertiary education degree (about 27% of the total migrant population in France) were over-qualified in the country, against less than 20% for the native-born working population (OECD and EU, 2015). The over-qualification rates are lower in the region of Île-de France both for natives and migrants compared to the national average but remain higher for migrants, reaching 12% for foreign-born and 8% for natives.

Often self-employment is a way into the labour market for migrants. The foreign population living in Paris is highly entrepreneurial. According to the 2016 Economic Atlas of Paris published by the *Greffe du Tribunal de Commerce de Paris*, 14% of companies established in Paris are headed by foreign residents and one out of ten companies is headed by a non-EU foreigner (APUR, 2016b) (see Figure 2.8). The most represented countries are Algeria (2.7% of all companies in Paris) and China (2.1%). It is in the east of Paris where the most companies headed by non-EU foreign nationals are located (e.g. 19.8% of the companies in the 20th arrondissement are headed by a non-EU foreigner). Yet, not all migrants have the vocation to be entrepreneurs or want to be entrepreneurs. Self-employment might sometimes be the only access to employment.

Figure 2.8. Origin of immigrant heads of companies in Paris, in 2016

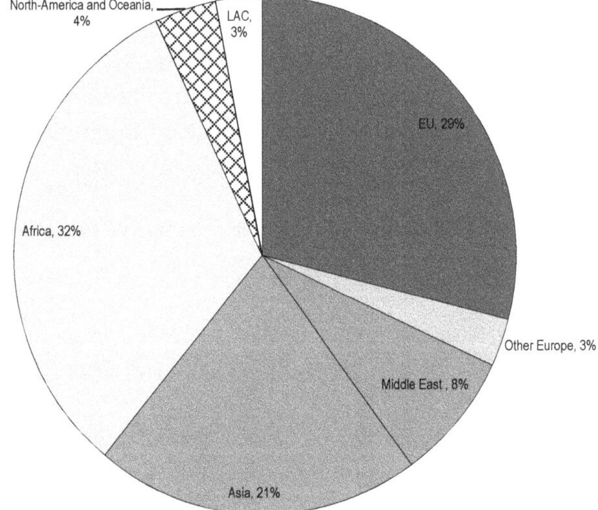

Source: OECD elaboration based on the 2016 *Economic Atlas of Paris*, published by the Greffe du Tribunal de Commerce de Paris.

Reasons for gaps in accessing the labour market

Among the reasons for the gaps in labour market integration that stakeholders had encountered included a poor command of the French language, particularly at the moment of entering the labour market. Even highly skilled and qualified migrants might struggle to develop their potential if they cannot communicate well with the host society (OECD and EU, 2015). This is an increasing barrier in France as the diversity of countries of origin of foreigners settling in France has progressively brought migrants from non-French-speaking countries. A diverse offer of language classes is accessible in the city of Paris as described in 2.4.4.

Labour market strategies implemented by the city in Paris

As all the rest of the population, regular migrants are entitled to unemployment benefits, job hunting and training services provided through the 900 employment agencies "*Pôle emploi*" spread out across the French Territory.

In addition, as a department and a city, Paris also supports Parisian labour market integration. Migrants are users of these non-migrant targeted services, which include professional training and job hunting support services. Some Parisian initiatives include:

1. The ***Parisian Plan for Insertion through Work*** *(Plan parisien de l'insertion par l'emploi* 2020, hereafter referred as PPIE) (Mairie de Paris, 2015a) targets a population that has lost contact for a considerable period with the job market such as the long-term unemployed among which migrants are among the main beneficiaries. The programme was initiated in July 2015 and adopted in June 2016, it aims at providing professional training and subsidised job opportunities to 1 100 long-term unemployed individuals living in Paris every year. Under the Paris Employment Training initiative Paris also provides tailored professional training and qualification services to 2 000 residents every year including migrants (Mairie de Paris, 2016).
2. The ***Parisian Pact to Fight Great Exclusion*** which underlines the city's commitment to support innovative labour market integration solutions such as the "first hour" scheme, which enables homeless people to progressively re-enter the job market through hour-based work contracts or the "*Lulu dans ma rue*" project, which provides the unemployed population of Paris with self-employment opportunities to offer local services to neighbours.
3. Set up in 2005 as part of the city's place-based approach to integration, the *North -Eastern Paris Local Plan for Integration and Employment* (PLIE) coordinates and develops synergies between the different initiatives for economic integration at the district level. Currently implemented in 9 Parisian districts (10th, 11th, 12th, 13th, 14th, 17th, 18th, 19th and 20th arrondissements) in neighbourhoods targeted by the City Policy in which migrants are overrepresented, this platform mobilises the private sector by providing tailored assistance to job seekers living in these districts in line with the skill needs of the employers and economic specificities of the territories.
4. Paris also supports specific initiatives for women regarding labour market integration and gender equality in the workplace. In 2016, spending in this area amounted to EUR 3 136 503 (Mairie de Paris, 2016) and were for example directed to non-profit organisations like ADAGE, which offers linguistic workshops and professional training to vulnerable women in the northern districts of Paris or to "*L'incubateur au féminin, Paris pionnières*", which supports female entrepreneurs (Mairie de Paris, 2016).

Activities targeting youth access to the labour market

Specific youth employment services are provided by the Ministry of Labour and Employment through the 445 "local missions" spread across the country. In Paris the Local Mission has 8 offices in the City-Policy areas and help 20 000 young people (16 to 25-year-old) every year. It is managed by a non-governmental partner organisation supported with EU, Prefecture and municipal funds and operates within a multiannual framework negotiated with the national level and in partnership with local Pôle emploi[19]. The local missions provide job -hunting services and inform about yearlong professional trainings and apprenticeship programmes, as well as youth-specific subsidises employment contracts. Furthermore, young people aged from 18 and 21-year-old, as well as unaccompanied minors, have access to the "young adult" facility which provides financial and technical support to young job seekers.

Targeted activities to accompany migrant and refugee labour market integration

Provided they have legal authorisation to work in France, economic migrants and refugees benefit from full access to the French job market and are entitled to job placement services provided by national and subnational public authorities. Asylum seekers, unlike other European countries such as Germany, Italy or Greece, which have recently reformed their approach, are not allowed to work in France[20]. This prohibition might slow integration as it entails long periods of inactivity, reliance on welfare assistance, distance with the host-society or may drag them into the informal sector if the allowances do not cover all their needs.

Throughout OECD meetings with Parisian and national stakeholders and as stated in the Taché report (see Section 2.1.1), French authorities recognise a need for "reinforced accompaniment" and targeted support for all persons with a permit to stay in France, in addition to equitable access to universal services for accessing the job market. In fact, both at the national and sub-national level, specific integration policies and initiatives are set up for migrants and refugees and they are likely to increase as a result of the Inter-ministerial Integration council (CII) of June 2018, presented in the paragraph on the evolution of integration policies paragraph 2.1.1 (Comité interministériel á l'intégration, 2018[2]). The CII recognised that integration policy needs to be territorialised "migrant integration must take into account the characteristics of each territory in terms of shortage of specific profiles s in the local labour market, vocational training available, housing solutions, etc. Thus more means will be made available at the local level. In particular EUR 20 million (*Fonds de soutien pour l'animation des territories*) will be put at the disposal of the Prefects to implement integration measures in this field, either through the departments or directly publishing calls for proposals. This funding is thought for mobilising local civil society alongside existing initiatives of local authorities.

For instance, since January 2017, according to national legislation, young unemployed francophone migrants (18 to 25-year-old) with adequate work permit can request financial assistance and tailored professional trainings as part of the universal "Youth Guarantee Scheme" (*Garantie Jeunes*) managed by Local Missions. Thanks to the partnership with the OFII which provided its expertise and to the funding provided by the National Museum of the History of

Immigration, the Parisian Local Mission tailored in 2017 a specific "Youth Guarantee Scheme" to the needs of young refugees. Implemented in partnership with the largest employer federation in France (MEDEF) this professionalising training for young refugees includes 50 hours of professionalising French, 330 hours of professional training and 70 hours of internship in companies[21].

Between 2018 and 2019, the CII aims at offering to 8 000 recently arrived young foreigners an opportunity for linguistic and socio-professional training during 3 to 6 months through the local missions. This training will be preparatory to universal measures to access labour market such as professional training and the *Garantie Jeunes*.

In particular for refugee public, the CII committed to providing to 5 000 refugees specific measures fostering labour market integration in the next few years. The measures will work along the lines of the HOPE project (see box 2.4) and will be implemented through territorial calls for proposals. In addition, in order to better match enterprises needs and refugees competences and to sensitize employers to employment and integration of refugees, the Inter-ministerial Delegate for reception and integration of refugees organised a workshop with private actors in June 2018 to encourage public-private partnership that foster refugees inclusion.

Box 2.5. HOPE: An initiative for refugee labour market integration

Since October 2017 the HOPE (*Hébergement orientation parcours vers l'emploi*) project involved 1 000 refugees (100 in Île-de France) in a dual 8 month language and work training. This innovative experience was implemented by the Association for the Professional Training of Adults (AFPA), in collaboration with the Ministry of Interior, the FAF TT, the French Public Employment Agency (Pôle emploi) and companies of temporary work (Addeco and Humando). The goal is to enable them to acquire qualifications in three fields: construction, services and industries. Many of the refugees trained through an internship in an enterprise have been offered a contract (Birschem, 2017).

Source: Authors' elaboration.

Paris responses for migrant and refugee integration in the labour market

As part of the Paris City Contract for the City Policy (2015-2020), the department provides financial support to non-profit organizations that promote migrant employment. In 2016, a total of EUR 610 000 was allocated to 40 projects in this area and benefited 1 600 people.

Paris has also developed strong networks with the private sector including with non-profit actors to foster migrant employment, professional training and entrepreneurship initiatives.

For instance, an initiative to foster access to the labour market for immigrant children and members of the so-called second generation is the Forum For Diversity and First Employment, which targets young job-seekers who are exposed to discrimination risks. In addition, districts (*arrondissements*) organise network initiatives with the private sector: the 12th arrondissement supported training for employers in non-discriminatory practices to support the recruitment of young migrants.

Further, the city also provides financial assistance to non-profit organisations and social businesses that support refugees' entrepreneurship and vocational training. For instance, the city funds SINGA France, an association supporting refugees' settlement, entrepreneurship and cultural integration. It also works to create synergies between refugees and their host communities. Besides cultural dialogue programmes and language classes, the NGO specifically focuses on creating job opportunities for refugees. As many refugees lack professional contacts, SINGA aims to connect them with relevant people who could help them set up their own business or find a job. In 2017, the city of Paris provided EUR 80 000 in financing to create a co-working space called "Kiwanda" that is managed by SINGA and the association Coexister working on intercultural matters. Since SINGA's creation in 2013, the NGO has accompanied entrepreneur refugees and in 2016 the NGO created the incubator "Finkela" for refugees aiming to develop an entrepreneurial or cultural project. In 2017, the organisation accompanied 300 refugees towards entrepreneurship for six months; so far 23% of them have reached financial autonomy after taking part in SINGA's programme. Among the incubated projects *Thot* (A language school for refugees), Meet My Mama (a food-catering company managed by refugee women) or AFM (a rap group).

Created in the 2016, *Action emploi réfugiés* (AER) is a platform that supports refugees' integration in the labour market by connecting refugees with employers through an online platform. Along with this matching mechanism, AER accompanies refugees before and after recruitment to secure labour market integration over time. AER also supports employers in hiring refugees through intercultural talks, awareness-raising activities about asylum law and mental health problems that refugees can face. Likewise, this association also informs and communicates to the general public about asylum and refuge topics (e.g. benefits to recruit refugees, legal specificities of refugees etc.). AER meets and works with the Parisian municipality on occasion, yet its funding comes solely from private foundations and Corporate Social Responsibility budgets. This limits its sustainability as they cannot plan initiatives in the long term. This two-year-old association has already helped 200 refugees to find a job.

2.4.2. Objective 10: Secure access to adequate housing

Access to adequate housing as a bottleneck for integration

Access to decent housing is an essential aspect of migrants' well-being and successful integration. Poor-quality and instable housing conditions tend to be associated with lower educational attainment, higher risk of social exclusion and poorer health status (Salvi del Pero et al., 2016).

In France, migrants tend to face poorer housing conditions than natives. They have relatively low rates of property ownership – 45% of migrants own their own homes against 62% for natives – and they are more likely to live in overcrowded and poor-quality housing conditions (OECD and EU, 2015). Such differences in overcrowding rates can be partially attributed to a higher average household size for migrants. For example, in the region of Île-de-France migrant households were on average, composed of 2.9 people in 2012 while the average household size for natives was 2.2 members according to INSEE.

Migrants in France also tend to be more overburdened by the cost of housing compared with native-born households, which can force households to cut back on other needs, including health care (Salvi del Petro et al., 2016). In Paris, migrants are also over-represented among the homeless population accounting for 76% of the total homeless population in 2015 (APUR, 2017c). This trend is partially attributed to their lack of economic resources and the official documents they need when arriving in the host country (Yaouancq and Duee, 2014). Since 2015 and the peak in arrivals, the number of migrants living in spontaneous camps through the city and in particular in the northeast has increased. As of March 2018, around 1 900 migrants were estimated to be living in such conditions in Paris (Baumard, 2018). Some of them are asylum seekers who cannot access the French asylum system because they have been registered in other EU countries under Dublin regulations, and others cannot be sheltered in the national reception system because of its limited accommodation capacities. According to the questionnaire filled out by the municipality for the preparation of this case study, lack of permanent housing for migrants and lack of shelters are the greatest difficulties faced in Paris for migrant integration.

Housing measures for migrant integration

As Parisian residents, migrants can have access the housing allowances and social-subsidized housing units provided by the French state and Paris (both as a city and a department).

Housing allowances

Provided they hold a valid residence permit, economic migrants and refugees have access to three different types of housing allowances provided by the French state under the Family Allowance Fund (*Caisse d'allocations familiales – CAF*): 1) the individualised housing allowance which supports poor tenants and home owners; 2) the family allowance supporting households with children; 3) the social housing allowance. In 2015, 379 645 people benefited from these three housing allowances in the city of Paris - about 17% of the city's total population (CAF, 2016). Applications for housing allowances can be completed online or at the 3 Parisian CAF centres and the 20 Parisian Centres for Social Action (CASVP).

As a Department, Paris also allocates a Housing Solidarity Fund (FSL) which provides financial aid for housing purposes to poor residents, including by incurring the costs related to house deposits, real estate agency fees and settlement. These assistance requests are handled by the Centres for Social Action of the City (CASVP). The Fund also supports organisations that implement housing integration initiatives in the territory.

The city of Paris, through its Centres for Social Action CASVP, also provides additional financial support for specific housing needs including electricity and housing improvements for impoverished people, families, single-parent families, elderly people and people with disabilities living in Paris for at least three years (*Paris aides au logement*). The homeless population of Paris can find emergency housing solutions through the municipal Permanent Social Assistance offices. The city also supports non -profit organisations such as Emmaus and les Enfants du Canal, to identify and redirect homeless people to the city's social services.

Emergency housing

All publics can access the centralised system for emergency shelter in Paris by calling the number for health emergencies "115". This service is managed by the SAMU Social of Paris, a municipal emergency service, a public interest group which allows public and private actors to coordinate. The service represents an example of coordination between associations and the public administration. It is organised across levels of government - Prefecture (DRIHL), Municipality (CASVP) and Department as well as a Federations of NGOs. The SAMU Social centralised the SIAO-Urgence which is the integrated service for reception and orientation that receives homeless or poorly-housed individuals. The SAMU-social de Paris centralises the information about available spots across all the shelters managed by partner associations and municipal entities. After the increase of arrivals in 2015, the Samu Social was crucial for refugee reception and re-direction to accommodation facilities yet it is operating at full capacity.

Access to social housing

France has a long history of social housing. The demand for social housing in Paris is quite high due to considerable pressure on the private real estate market. In 2017, housing prices increased by 8.6% in Paris.[22] The Centres for Social Action and Permanent Social Assistance offices support Parisian residents in their application for social housing. As of December 2015, 219 532 households requested social housing in Paris. In their request, 26% of households indicated that they would prefer a housing solution outside of Paris. According to the Parisian Direction for Housing and Habitat, half of the requests were rehoused within a year.

Social housing is a shared competence in Paris mainly between the national level and the Ville de Paris (communal and department level). The housing institutional setting in Île-de-France and Paris is known as entangled (IAU, 2012). There are two key actors in social housing: Rightful actors and Manager actors. Rightful actors ("*réservataires*") are those who contribute to the financing or rehabilitation of social housing and thus are entitled with reservation rights to social housing units ("contingents"). In the Parisian territory, the city of Paris is the first rightful organism controlling 34.2% of the social housing stock followed by social housing companies (mostly Paris Habitat) (22.9% of the social housing stock) and the state (i.e. DRIHIL and Prefecture de Police) which has rights over 21% of the social housing stock. The other organisms with reservation rights over social housing are Action Logement (private employers) (12.6%), associations (7.9%) and the region (less than 1%) (Apur, 2013). Social housing is run by Social Housing companies called "*Bailleurs sociaux*" in French which are the Manager actors (e.g. Paris Habitat, RIVP, Immobilière 3F). To allocate social housing, the social housing company alerts the relevant rightful actor of the availability, which then proposes three registered candidates. The manager actor makes the final decision in an Attribution Commission. The Mayor of Paris and the mayor of the relevant arrondissement are represented on this Attribution Commission as so can the Prefect if requested. After the consent of the Commission, the retained candidate can access the allocated social housing unit. The city's approach to social housing is of general provision to its population regardless of their origin. In France, migrants can have access to social housing once they have residency status.

National legislation[23] requires French cities to render available 20% of their housing stock for social housing (percentages between 20% and 25% and implementation of the law are related to municipal size and location). Since 2013, Paris needs to reach a 25% quota by 2025. If they fail to reach the legal quota, local authorities are subject to a fine. As of January 2016, 19.9% of the housing stock in Paris was targeted for social housing (APUR, 2017b). In the case of Paris, each district (arrondissement) needs to comply with the national law contributing to reduce spatial segregation. The municipal Direction for Housing and Habitat, is committed to improving the distribution of social housing within the city, which has historically been highly uneven (see 1.2).

The city of Paris has made social housing a priority and set the ambitious objective of creating 7 500 new units per year for the whole population (including migrants) and aims to reach a level of 30% of the Parisian housing stock by 2030. 7 502 new units of social housing were added in Paris in 2016, the highest number since 2001 (vs. 7 388 in 2015).

Concerning the expansion of its social real estate, Paris has a multimodal policy. Indeed, given the high density of the city, constructing new buildings is challenging within city limits. Consequently, 30.2% of new social housing units were built, while 8.4% were bought from the private market and renovated and the remaining 61.3% were bought without renovation.

Foyers travailleurs migrants (FTM) (Residences for Migrants workers) are social housing solutions created in the mid-1950s to accommodate north-African workers. In Paris there are 26 FTM. None of them are used to house newcomers (asylum seekers and refugees); instead they are occupied by more longstanding migrants. These residences offer permanent accommodation to regular migrants living alone and who work in France. Since 2005, management of the FTMs shifted from the central government to the municipality (Direction for Housing and Habitat and the City Policy Delegate). The municipality outsourced the management to housing associations (ADOMA, Coalia, Lerichemonnt[24]. Between 2005 and 2016, 4 140 housing units were renovated (Mairie de Paris, 2016). In addition, 1 000 new housing units were created to respond to heightened demand for individual housing units.

Seeking alternatives for affordable housing in the city, the municipality of Paris launched in 2007 the programme *Louez solidaire sans risque* – Solidarity Rent without Risk. Through this programme, the city refurbishes, offers guaranteed rent and fiscal incentives to private landlords who lease their properties to the municipality who will use it for vulnerable populations including migrants. The programme is financed by the city and implemented in collaboration with the partner association SOLIHA which supports private landlords who sign up for the program. This programme not only increases the number of properties available for social housing but also avoids concentration in specific neighbourhoods as it exploits existing housing stock across the city. In 2015, *Louez solidaire sans risque* had reached 2 900 people in 902 units and the programme has been replicated in several other French cities (see Figure 2.9).

Figure 2.9. The municipal programme « Louez Solidaire Sans Risque »

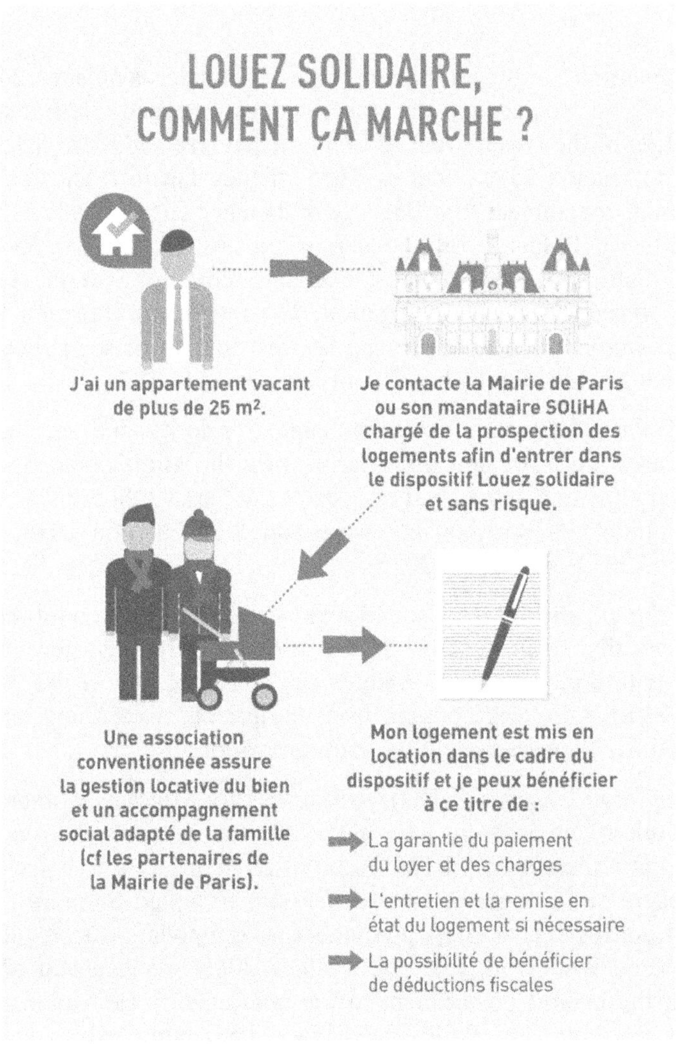

Source: https://www.paris.fr/louezsolidaire.

Urban planning and long-term housing solutions

The city is driven by the aspiration to reinvent spaces and initiatives through participative processes. *Réinventer Paris* (Reinvent Paris) is the first call for innovative urban projects (APUI) organised by the city of Paris (*Direction de l'urbanisme*). Since 2014, the city identified among its properties, some sites (buildings, lands, etc.) for sale to private actors and opened a public bid to identify the most innovative proposals. 22 sites have been awarded through this process and have been sold in September 2016 for a total of EUR 565 million (APUR, 2017d). One of the main selection criteria was the multi-functionality of the buildings: spaces must respond to different needs and be attractive for different publics, offering at the same time housing and cultural solutions. Among other projects also the *Grands Voisins* (see Section 2.2.2) the old hospital (Saint Vincent de Paul), will be transformed from temporary housing solution for 600 persons into an eco-neighbourhood. The hybrid project combining temporary housing for refugees and offices for resident entrepreneurs resulted in a new space for socialisation in the neighbourhood. The current shared governance model of the space –between three associations, the municipality and the prefecture- proved effective in creating an atypical space "where everyone could feel welcome and legitimate" (APUR 2017d). Integrating the lessons learned from this experience, the project for the upcoming eco-neighbourhood evolved over time. From an almost exclusively residential project it will now involve a permanent accommodation centre for refugees (50-100 places) and offices that will be rent at low rates to attract actors engaged in the social and solidarity[25].

Specific housing measures for refugees

As reflected in the Paris 18-point plan "Mobilisation of the Community of Paris to welcome refugees" (Mairie de Paris, 2015b), the city and department of Paris have committed to providing specific housing services to newly arrived migrants, with a focus on the vulnerable population. For this purpose, new shelter facilities (e.g. a centre in Bourg-la-Reine with 50 units available for women with children, *Les Grands Voisins*) were created to receive newcomers, as well as the two CPAs in La Chapelle and Ivry described in Section 2.2.1. Before the creation of the CPAs, 30 temporary shelters housed 23 000 people in the city mobilising civil servants from the city and the Prefecture as well as NGOs. In April 2015, the council of Paris enacted the new department reception and housing mechanisms for unaccompanied minors. Within the Parisian departmental services for youth protection (DASES), the new facility provides comprehensive support to unaccompanied minors, especially with regard to legal procedures, health care and educational needs. Specific sheltering support and services for pregnant women and women with children have also been provided in partnership with non-profit organisations. Yet, as mentioned previously makeshift camps persist in the city's outskirts and migrant homelessness remains a serious issue, including for unaccompanied minors.

Further, the national level has recently engaged in providing housing solutions for refuges (see Box 2.).

Box 2.6. National approach for refugee housing solutions

Refugee access to housing is essential for their integration and calls for a local approach due to territorial disparities in social housing availability and housing affordability. With regards to social housing for refugees, at the national level, co-signed by the Interior and the Territorial Cohesion Ministers, a 12 December 2017 instruction calls for an increased mobilisation of all relevant actors (local authorities, public services, '*bailleurs socieux*', NGOs and private sector) to improve access to housing for refugees with a target of 20 000 housing units by the end of 2018. *Préfets* are responsible for implementing this national instruction at the regional level by ensuring balanced distribution of refugees among *départements*.

2 500 among these 20 000 units should be mobilised through the national platform for refugee housing established since 2015 by the Interministerial delegation for temporary accommodation and access to housing (*Délégation interministérielle à l'hébergement et à l'accès au logement*, DIHAL). In 2015, DIHAL developed a platform to respond to the housing needs of relocated and reinstalled refugees. This task adds to its mandate to accompany beneficiaries of social housing. Refugees are considered a priority public and can benefit from all sorts of social housing (not only national government social housing units but also from other owners) (Dihal, 2017; Tache, 2018). The DIHAL platform works in close collaboration with local authorities in matching those refugees accepting geographical mobility with vacancies in both public and private housing in areas with lower housing demand –outside of Île-de-France.

In addition to housing, refugees benefit from integration measures to find work and access education. The municipal Centres for Social Action CCAS (i.e. equivalent to the CASVP in other French municipalities) as well as local associations provide these services in partnership with the DIHAL. Around 5 200 people have benefited from the platform since 2015. In addition, DIHAL, in collaboration with Pôle Emploi, is elaborating a national online platform matching employment offers and social housing spots available in the national territory. While not only addressed to migrants or refugees, this initiative might be used by these publics as well, especially when not attached to a territory and willing to relocated anywhere in France (DIHAL, 2017).

Source: Authors' elaboration.

Temporarily accommodating refugees in private houses

In Paris, a mechanism for short-term housing in private homes was created building on the civil society solidarity response in 2015. ELAN is a pluridisciplinary mechanism to secure refugee housing in private homes along with social, sanitary and professional support by experienced associations. ELAN was managed by the SAMU Social and was financed by the foundation of a private bank (BNP Paribas). Following this initiative, the DIHAL is implementing at the national level a similar project and financed eleven associations to identify and select households wanting to receive refugees at home on a voluntary basis and support both sides. This experimental project aims at hosting 1 000 refugees in two years, and to accommodate refugees for periods lasting between three months and a year maximum.

2.4.3. Objective 11: Provide social welfare measures that are aligned with migrant inclusion

Social services and welfare measures

France is the OECD country with the highest public social spending to GDP ratio, at over 30%. In Paris, "Social support and solidarity" is the second biggest expenditure (23%) in the 2017 operating budget of the city – after administrative costs – and is estimated at EUR 1 365 million (Mairie de Paris, 2017).

As mentioned in Section 2.2.1, as part of its integration strategy, Paris makes efforts for adapting its public services to migrant characteristics for facilitating their access over time. This does not take the form of specialised social service hubs for migrants as is the case in other cities analysed. More often, the integration budget is used to make sure universal services are adapted to this group, for instance by providing translation services at the CASV and offering training to municipal officers in each district on how to receive a public with a foreign background. In particular, the city is concerned with digital inclusion and deploys 'digital mediators' who accompany users in accessing digital public services and applications for welfare benefits. This service is designed to help vulnerable people, often homeless migrants in their interaction with public services.

As mentioned (Section 2.3.1) the city is engaged to better adapting its services to the needs of migrant groups. However, from OECD interviews with municipal officers it emerged that the city could better organise this ambition by connecting all the actors involved through an operational strategy. The 2015's 18 points plan is an example of vision for refugee integration across city directorates, which does not exist for migrant. See Section 2.1.2 for a more in-depth analysis of policy coherence for integration policy. According to one of the testimonies collected, by better responding to migrants' needs the city would innovate also in the way it responds to the general public and achieve better results.

Box 2.7. CASVP one of the key actors providing public social services to all groups including migrants

The CASVP is the Centre for Social Action of the City of Paris. Is a public operational agency that responds to the needs of the most vulnerable which receives different sources of funding. With 7 000 staff, it is the biggest budget of the city of Paris. As described in section 2.1.2, almost 50% of the budget for the city's integration strategy (EUR 28 million) is spent through the 20 Centres for Social Action (CASVP). CASVP are key providers of universal social services and they support with financial allowance and accessing social rights and accommodation. All persons with at least three years residency are eligible to CASVP services. For instance, since 2005, the CASVP made its supplemental assistance (*aides facultatives* which support vulnerable groups on top of the other allowances made available by national mechanisms) also available to non-EU citizens under the same conditions of all other users. Further, CASVP also provides migrant-specific support such as translation services with a budget of EUR 73 000 in 2016.

Recently the CASVP noticed an increase in the number of refugees using the three Social Reception centres (*Permanences sociale d'accueil* - PSA) that they manage in the city. These reception hubs receive and accompany homeless people in accessing their social rights (e.g. living allocation, health card, family allocation, etc.). According to OECD interviews with the CASV around 70% of PSA users in 2017 were protection status holders. Most of these refugees had never been hosted in one of the reception centres for asylum seekers (CADA) (see Section 2.1.4) thus might not have received sufficient support and information with regards to accessing their social rights during this phase. Before the 2015 peak in arrival the CASVP was in charge of managing 4 CHU (*Centre d'hebergement d'urgence*), in their experience 50% of the public was composed by irregular migrants (OECD interviews with CASVP).

Source: Authors' elaboration.

Welfare benefits for migrants and refugees

As Parisian residents, regular migrants and refugees have access to welfare benefits provided by the French State, the department and city of Paris, which are allocated according to vulnerability criteria. There is one exception to this universal rule which is the RSA Revenu de Solidarité Active (RSA- Minimum Active Income). This minimum income to which only over 25-year-old residents have access, is only accessible to non-EU migrants once they have held a work permit for five years, whereas refugees have direct access to the RSA[28].

While the general principle is that citizens should provide for themselves through work, a minimum revenue for citizens with insufficient income is provided by the state (RSA). Within the metropolitan area of Paris it is calculated that social welfare allowances have reduced by 44% income inequalities between richer and poor households (Apur, 2017a).

The RSA is managed by the department level and allocated by the CAF. The city of Paris is aware of the general difficulties in accessing the RSA and aims at modernising its organisation (Mairie de Paris, 2015a). On average, there is a 100-day delay between the start of the administrative process and when the individual can actually exercise his or her right to the RSA. This bottleneck is partially due to the multitude of partner actors involved (currently more than seven different services are in charge of accompanying the RSA public and allocating the benefit distributed by the department: Pôle emploi, CAF, Espaces parisiens d'insertion, Service Social Polyvalent, etc.). A simplified organisation would accelerate the process and avoid disruptions in the social inclusion processes. The city of Paris has set the objective of a 30-day delay by 2020.

This benefit is not accessible for specific categories of migrants: women who have entered the country through family reunification systems cannot access the RSA until five years after their arrival, which could curb their autonomy.

Protection towards vulnerable migrants and refugees

Paris, as a department, is responsible for supporting vulnerable residents such as unaccompanied minors, isolated women and women with children.

Unaccompanied minors benefit from children protection mechanisms – a departmental competence. A Parisian plan for the reception and support of unaccompanied foreign minors was adopted in April 2015. In 2016, 30% of the more than 4 900 minors supported by the Department of Paris were migrant unaccompanied minors or young adults, (Mairie de Paris, 2015b). The city has established a mechanism to provide them with unconditional shelter and has tripled the number of spots during 2016 to respond to the increasing number of unaccompanied minors arriving. The municipality also created a specific process to rapidly identify and orient homeless unaccompanied minor migrants towards protection services. From OECD interviews with third sector stakeholders, it emerged that further collaboration with civil society associations and citizens would be necessary given the high number of unaccompanied minors who remain isolated and unprotected. Paris is also engaged with the protection of women – particularly when pregnant or accompanied by children. A support mechanism and systematic shelter is established thanks to the collaboration of the city and its partners.

Access to health care

Access to health care is managed between the National Health Minister and the Regional Health Agencies (ARS) which are deconcentrated entities of the central government in regions. In France, health costs are divided into the compulsory part (reimbursed by social security) and the "*complémentaire*" supplemental part (paid by the patient or reimbursed by supplementary health insurance for low-income individuals).

Regular migrants who have lived in France for more than three months can benefit from Universal Health Protection through the PUMA, which covers the compulsory health cost in case of disease or maternity. In case of low-income revenues, regular migrants can also access the CMU-C which is a free, supplemental health insurance policy that covers the cost of the "*complémentaire*" part. Undocumented migrants can access AME (*Aide médicale d'État*) under certain conditions (i.e. revenues, lack of documents and more than 3 months in the country) which is valid for a year (and renewable) and covers 100% of medical consultations. To avoid obstacles for migrant woman when accessing health care during a pregnancy, the municipality pays costs in case the bureaucratic procedures for universal care protection are not yet finalised.

Further, the PASS (*Permanence d'accès aux soins de santé)* plays an important role for access to health care for vulnerable migrants (e.g. asylum seekers and undocumented migrants). It was created in 1998 to "fight exclusions" and promote "equality between all people" and was thought as providing a transitory access before obtaining a formalized healthcare (PUMA).

The city of Paris also has 5 Municipal Health Centres (CMS) that offer health care and prevention services (e.g. disseminate information, vaccine adjustments, medical screening, etc.) that are also used by migrants. With the objective of reaching individuals who have less access to health information the city of Paris has established a mobile service for health information and prevention (EMIP) which reaches, in particular, migrant residence houses (FTA). In addition, at the PMI Maternal Child Protection units, which are a departmental competence, mediation services are offered. These services, outsourced to three associations for a total of EUR 125 000 in 2016, facilitate linguistic and cultural mediation with families with foreign background.

However, these approaches are not resolving the quantity and complexity of migrant health needs and more needs to be done to address this issue.

2.4.4. Objective 12: Establish education responses to address segregation and provide equitable paths to professional growth

While most migrants receive their initial education in their country of origin, the host country can play a significant role in enhancing migrant educational level and qualifications to match the requirements of its labour market, especially with regard to language skills development and access to tertiary education (OECD and EU, 2015). In 2014-15, migrants were on average less educated than the native-born population in the Île-de-France region. For instance, more than two thirds of migrants living in Île-de-France do not hold a tertiary education degree while almost half of natives are highly educated (Table 2.2).

Table 2.2. Educational attainment of foreign -born relative to native-born in the region of Île-de-France 2914-2015

% low-educated	% medium-educated	% highly-educated	% low-educated	% medium-educated	% highly-educated
15	37	47		27	32

Source: OECD database on immigrant integration at the regional level 41.

In France, school programmes and teachers are a competence of the national government through the National Ministry of Education. As a municipality, however, Paris is responsible for the logistics and maintenance of primary schools, and as a department, of the secondary schools (*collèges*). Education represented 9% of the operating budget in 2017 or EUR 721 million. Most of municipal expenditures support teaching services, including cafeteria costs. In 2017, the city spent around EUR 23 million for extracurricular activities for maternal and elementary schools[29], including on Wednesdays and Saturdays when there are no regular classes.

Jointly with the national government, the city has made it a priority to universalise access to school for all pupils residing in the territory and to assess the local needs of students who do not speak French as a first language. The Parisian Territorial Education Project 2016-2019 (PETP, 2015) established education guidelines for the 2016-2019 period in Paris. It is elaborated in coordination between the municipality (DASCO), the CAF and the National Ministry of Education (through the *Préfecture* and *Rectorat*).

Access to school for recently arrived children and young adults

The city manages the reception and inclusion of children and young adults who do not speak French or from Roma communities - in schooling age through the centre CASNAV (*Centre académique pour la scolarisation des enfants allophones nouvellement arrivés et des enfants issus de familles itinérants et de voyageurs*). The centre supervises and assists the schooling of newly arrived children who do not speak French (i.e. access to school, specific pedagogical resources, teacher training). The CASNAV orientates allophone children and young adults towards "UPE2A" classes.

"UPE2A" is a tailor-made temporary initiative within the school system for migrant children to learn French. UPE2A "Pedagogic Units for Allophone recently arrived pupils" (*Unités pédagogiques pour élèves allophones arrivants*) are temporary classes addressed to non-French speaker pupils recently arrived in France regardless of their parents' administrative situation. These classes are seen as gateways and their main objective is language learning (18 hours of French per week) to allow integration into a regular class of the pupil's age as soon as possible. In Paris there are 50 classes in elementary schools and 40 in middle schools.

It can also be noted that in February 2017, a school opened within a refugee shelter (CHU) in Ivry-sur-Seine. Thanks to the close collaboration of the CASNAV of Paris and the neighbouring city of Ivry along with the municipality of Paris and the NGO Emmaus managing the CHU, the school belongs to the national education system and provides lessons to 70 pupils.

While effective in learning the language quickly, ad-hoc schooling systems for pupils with a migration background might result in segregated classes where students have a lower education performance compared to the city average (European Commission, 2018, Toolkit on the use of EU funds for the integration of people with a migrant background). Other cities (Barcelona, Gothenburg, etc.) try to strengthen pedagogical tools (i.e. active and collaborative approaches to increase pupils' motivation, individual support and language training, continuous professional development for education professionals, etc.) available in standard classes to address different needs of students with a migrant background.

The school system as leverage for parent integration

The school system in Paris is seen as a way to integrate the entire migrant family in addition to providing educational instruction to their children. The programme "Open the school to parents for children success" (*Ouvrir l'école aux parents pour la réussite des enfants* - OPRE) allows schools to organise classes for non-EU migrant parents on a voluntary basis. The content of the OPRE classes ranges from language learning, follow up of their child's education and understanding French Republican values (PETP, 2015). This mechanism plays a double role of strengthening the integration into the school system of UPE2A (see paragraph above) children and their family's broader integration into society. There are 120 hours per school year and attending parents receive a certificate. The programme is financed by the national government through the ministry of National Education and the Interior ministry. In the school year 2013-2014, 567 parents benefited from this programme in Paris. The city invests through associations such as Culture 2+ in actions facilitating relations between non-francophone families and the school. For instance, *papothéques* (Spaces for chat) are opportunities for parents from a same linguistic and cultural community to meet with school teachers and directors in the presence of social worker, translator and school psychologists to exchange in their mother tongue.

Priority Education Areas to reduce segregation

In France, the "*carte scolaire*" (school maps) matchs the schools where parents can register their children based on proximity to where they live. This potentially reproduces segregation patterns as rich neighbourhood residents are more likely to access schools with better outcomes than City Policy residents.

The Priority Education system is a national French Policy to address the impact of socio-economic and territorial inequalities on children's school results. The mechanism strengthens pedagogical action in schools in the most socio-economically disadvantaged neighbourhoods in which migrants are overrepresented. Since the last reform of City Policy geography, Priority Education schools converge with Priority Neighbourhoods targeted by the City Policy. The criterion determining Priority Education is set by the National Education Ministry and includes the socio-professional category of the parents, the percentage of scholarship holders and of residents of City Policy neighbourhoods. Priority Education schools can be either REP *(Réseaux d'éducation prioritaire)* and the most disadvantaged centres are REP+ *(Réseau d'éducation prioritaire +)*. In Paris, Priority Education involves 25 *collèges* for pre-teens (25 in REP and 4 in REP+) and 215 elementary schools (187 in REP and 28 in REP+) (PETP, 2015). A 2017 reform targeted the most socially disadvantaged six and seven-year-old children by doubling the number of their classes in Priority Education Schools[26]. In Paris, this reform concerned the schools of the most deprived neighbourhoods (e.g.13th, 18th, 19th, 20th) which are also the areas with the highest percentage of migrants and foreigners (see Figure 2.10).

Figure 2.10. Priority schools benefiting from the doubling of CP-CEI classes

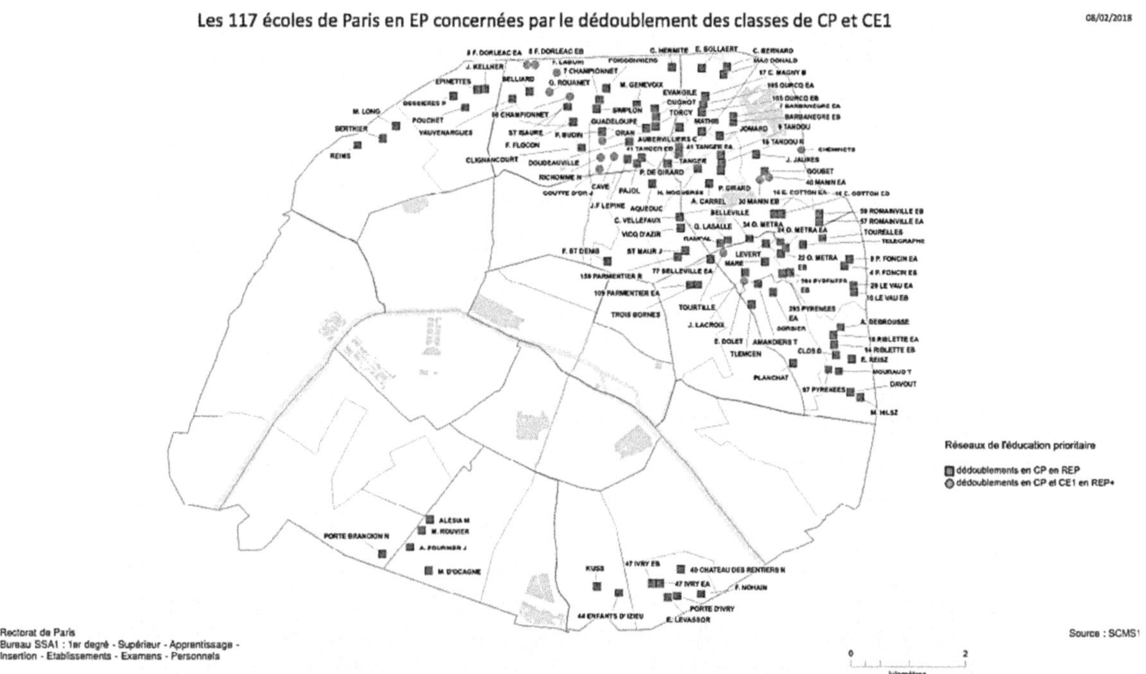

Note: CP (classe préparatoire) and CE1 (classe élementaire 1) are the first two grades of the elementary school in France corresponding to 6-7 year old children.
Source: PETP; Projet éducatif territorial de Paris (2015), Projet éducatif territorial de Paris 2016-2019.

Access to higher education

Paris is a European higher education hub with 370 higher education centres among which 12 universities and 450 000 students enrolled.

Some Parisian universities (e.g. Sciences-Po Paris, Paris Dauphine, Université Paris 1 Panthéon – Sorbonne) volunteered for facilitating refugee integration by creating specific pedagogical programmes to enable refugees with a high school diploma, to take their courses. These programmes mostly consist in a combination of French language acquisition programmes and peer-support systems or "buddy programmes". Through these programmes the students are exempted from tuition and fees and receive support to complete the administrative procedures.

The Centre for Universities and School (CROUS) is a national public service provider for students with local sub-divisions throughout the country, under the jurisdiction of the National Ministry of Education. The Parisian CROUS was mobilised to provide housing assistance and food for refugees participating in these university programs.

Language learning

At the local level, Paris considers language learning an essential domain for integration efforts and the municipality allocates subsidies to non-governmental organisations through calls for projects (Mairie de Paris, 2016). Their role is particularly crucial for language courses addressed to asylum seekers as they are not entitled to government courses.

The municipality subsidises free language courses. Since 2008, the city has headed up French language acquisition efforts and is managed by the Service of Equality, Integration and Inclusion (DDCT) with the support of the Direction of School Affaires (DASCO) for its expertise in the creation of training programmes. The city has provided EUR 7.7 million which have benefited up to 16 000 learners through actions carried out by six municipal directorates. The city provides socio-linguistic workshops, linguistic bridges and impoverished areas of the city - Priority Neighbourhoods - benefit from increased linguistic workshops.

Municipal courses for adults are addressed to people who struggle to express themselves in French. Further, the municipality orientates newcomers to associations financed by the municipality through subsidies. Partner associations have historically been and remain (Safi, 2009) key actors in the development of adult language courses in Paris especially for asylum seekers as they are not beneficiaries of government courses.

Indeed, at the national level, through the OFII, language courses are proposed as part of the Republican Integration Contract. As mentioned before (see 2.1.1), the Republican Integration Contract is signed between the State and all non-EU residents staying more than a year. Along with civic training, the CIR includes language courses given by the OFII, theoretically aiming to attain A1 level. After an initial language exam, which determines their level of proficiency, the OFFI assigns migrants to language courses delivered by 34 partner language schools and qualified organisations operating at the national level, which do not necessarily operate in contact with local authorities. There was a 50% increase in the OFII budget for language courses between 2016 and 2017 (EUR 46 million in 2017). During OECD interviews with stakeholders in Paris, some limits of the OFII language courses were signalled including (1) the lack of courses for asylum seekers; (2) heterogeneity of the language groups and lack of adaptation to qualification of participants; (3) insufficient number of class hours; (4) lack of link with specific professional sectors. Similar gaps have recently been indicated by national level representatives (Karoutchi, 2017; Taché, 2018). The recent National Strategy for Refugee Integration (See 2.1.4), partially takes into account such gaps by increasing the number of hours, creating courses for illiterate foreigners and developing language courses with professional content.

Specific municipal support is granted to courses for refugees and asylum seekers. As an example, in 2016, through a call for projects for language courses addressed to young refugees, the municipality financed two associations. Kiron France which gives language courses for students wanting to re-integrate the higher education system; and the association "Agros Migrateurs for students" wanting to join the engineering sector.

Further municipal support is allocated to professionalising language courses to facilitate migrant labour market integration. The municipality finances the association CEFIL (*Centre d'études de formation et d'insertion par la langue*) together with the national government (through the CGET budget for City Policy) and the European Union (FSE and AMF funds). CEFIL provides language courses specialised for migrant professional insertion in specific domains. Among these courses for instances the Restaur'Action teaches French and key skills to work in hotels and restaurants and Communic'Action teaches professional French for domestic workers.

To better respond to the sizeable needs in terms of language acquisition at the city level, the municipality (DASCO and DDCT) developed the platform EIF-FEL to enhance the coordination among language course providers. The aim of the EIF-FEL platform, overseen by two NGOs (CEFIL and Centre Alpha Choisy) aims at better orientating users of language courses to offers that match their needs, improve coherence among the courses and the evaluations provided in different centres.

Further, the booklet "Where to learn French in Paris" gathers all the information about the existing offers in Paris in a clear format.

Notes

1. This is the first time that France has a national public policy and budget clearly targeting racism and antisemitism, http://www.gouvernement.fr/plan-national-de-lutte-contre-le-racisme-et-l-antisemitisme-2018-2020.
2. http://www.gouvernement.fr/bilan-2017-des-actes-racistes-antisemites-antimusulmans-et-antichretiens.
3. Further information can be found at: http://www.senat.fr/rap/r16-660/r16-660_mono.html#toc22.
4. According to the OECD database on metropolitan areas, the perimeter of the metropole is smaller than the one of the Functional Urban Area of Paris (https://stats.oecd.org/Index.aspx?DataSetCode=CITIES.
5. Since 2013, priority geography only depends on the ratio of low income residents (concentration of poor households, weighted by the local fiscal income).
6. https://es.scribd.com/document/371844601/Rapport-de-Aurelien-Tache.
7. « Je souhaite promouvoir le Paris de la Fraternité par une politique active de lutte contre les discriminations. Paris est une ville mondiale d'immigration et de brassage de cultures. Tous différents, nous n'en restons pas moins tous Parisiens. Tout en reconnaissant à chacun son identité, il nous faut construire une identité collective inclusive. »
8. 28% of people living in City-Policy-targeted neighbourhoods are foreigners or have a migration background.
9. http://www.quiaccueillequi.org/fiches/public.php?pageNum_organismes=0&totalRows_organismes=43&colonne=Pers_I.
10. Centre of Social Action of the City of Paris.
11. https://co-city.fr/fr/pages/5-qui-sommes-nous.
12. The ADA represents monthly EUR 200 (or EUR 300 if the asylum seeker is not hosted in asylum -seeker accommodation facilities).
13. Further information can be found at: http://www.psmigrants.org/site/wp-content/uploads/2018/02/Typologie-des-dispositifs-dhébergements-contrôles.pdf.
14. http://france-terre-asile.org/images/stories/droit-refugies/emploi-formation/plaquette-reloref-2010/ftda-reloref-general.pdf.

15. The RSA is a minimum allowance for citizens with insufficient income provided by the State. It is managed by the department level and allocated by the CAF.
16. The RSA is a minimum allowance for citizens with insufficient income provided by the State. It is managed by the department level and allocated by the CAF.
17. Organisational barriers slow the production of residence permits (*titre de séjour*) for migrants, and residence cards for recognised refugees before they constitute their civil status. Due to these delays, migrants and refugees can spend over a year before receiving their residence permits.
18. Presentation of the 104: http://www.104.fr/presentation.html.
19. https://jemengage.paris.fr/.
20. http://www.quiaccueillequi.org/secourscatholique.php.
21. http://travail-emploi.gouv.fr/ministere/acteurs/service-public-de-l-emploi/article/missions-locales.
22. Asylum seekers can exceptionally receive an authorisation to work if after nine months of having claimed asylum, their status has not been decided by the OFPRA.
23. http://missionlocaledeparis.fr/garantie-jeunes-adapter-loffre-de-service-au-public-jeunes-refugies/.
24. http://immobilier.lefigaro.fr/article/a-paris-le-prix-moyen-des-logements-va-bientot-depasser-9300-euros-le-m2_5c37aea2-17b5-11e8-9a69-2c6c51585454/.
25. The SRU law (*Loi relative à la solidarité et au renouvellement urbain*) passed in 2000 highly modified urban and housing law in France by enforcing the stipulation that municipalities - of more than 1 500 inhabitants in Ile-de-France and more than 3 500 inhabitants elsewhere, within agglomerations of over 50 000 residents - have at least 20% social housing. This quota was increased to 25% in 2013 through the ALUR law.
26. http://annuaire.action-sociale.org/etablissements/readaptation-sociale/foyer-de-travailleurs-migrants-non-transforme-en-residence-sociale-256/rgn-ile-de-france/Organismes.html.
27. https://www.apur.org/fr/nos-travaux/ville-autrement-initiatives-citoyennes-urbanisme-temporaire-innovations-publiques.
28. The amount of the allowance depends on household composition and RSA beneficiaries' participation in a labour market integration programme (i.e. actively look for employment, engage in vocational training).
29. CP and CE1 classes are the grades corresponding to 6 and 7-year-old children in the French Primary School System.

References

APUR; Atelier parisien d'urbanisme (2017a), « La géographie des sans abri à Paris », *APUR* Note, No.115.

APUR; Atelier parisien d'urbanisme (2017b), « Métropole du Grand Paris : des écarts de revenus encore élevés malgré la redistribution », *APUR Note,* No.114.

APUR; Atelier parisien d'urbanisme (2017c), *Les chiffres du logement social à Paris en 2016.*

APUR; Atelier parisien d'urbanisme (2017d), La ville autrement, initiatives citoyennes, urbanisme temporaire, innovations publiques, plateformes numériques, https://www.apur.org/fr/nos-travaux/ville-autrement-initiatives-citoyennes-urbanisme-temporaire-innovations-publiques.

APUR; Atelier parisien d'urbanisme (2016a), *Les quartiers parisiens de la politique de la ville - Contrat de ville 2015-2020.*

APUR; Atelier parisient d'urbanisme (2016b), *Les entrepreneurs étrangers à Paris.*

APUR; Atelier parisien d'urbanisme (2013), *L'accès au logement social à Paris - Analyse de la demande de logement social et bilan des propositions et attributions de logements sociaux à Paris en 2012.*

APUR; Atelier parisien d'urbanisme (2011), *Sans-abri à Paris : La présence des sans-abris sur le territoire parisien et l'action de la collectivité pour aider à leur réinsertion.*

Baumard, M. (2018) Sur les trottoirs parisiens, près de 2000 migrants attendent de pouvoir déposer une demande d'asile , Lemonde.fr https://www.lemonde.fr/immigration-et-diversite/article/2018/04/03/sur-les-trottoirs-parisiens-pres-de-2-000-migrants-attendent-de-pouvoir-deposer-une-demande-d-asile_5279765_1654200.html

.

Birschem, N. (2017), « Avec l'Afpa, des réfugiés en route vers l'emploi », *La Croix.*

Boulant, J., M. Brezzi and P. Veneri (2016), *Income levels and inequality in metropolitan areas: A comparative approach in OECD countries*, OECD Publishing, Paris, http://dx.doi.org/10.1787/20737009.

Bouvier, G. (2012), *Vue d'ensemble : les descendants d'immigrés plus nombreux que les immigrés : une position française originale en Europe*, INSEE : Immigrés et descendants d'immigrés en France.

Brutel, C. (2017), *Etre né d'un parent immigré : une population diverse reflétant l'histoire des flux migratoires*, INSEE Première.

Brutel, C. (2016), *La localisation géographique des immigrés : Une forte concentration dans l'aire urbaine de Paris,* INSEE Première.

CAF (2016), *Personnes couvertes par une aide au logement en 2015*, CAF data (accessed December 2015).

Charbit, C. (2011), "Governance of Public Policies in Decentralised Contexts: The Multi-level approach", *OECD Regional Development Working Papers*, No. 2011/04, OECD Publishing, Paris, https://doi.org/10.1787/5kg883pkxkhc-en.

Charbit, C. and M. Michalun (2009), "Mind the gaps: Managing Mutual Dependence in Relations among Levels of Government", *OECD Working Papers on Public Governance*, No. 14, OECD Publishing, Paris, https://doi.org/10.1787/221253707200.

Charbit, C. and O. Romano (2017), "Governing together: an international review of contracts across levels of government for regional development", *OECD Regional Development Working Papers*, No. 2017/04, OECD Publishing, Paris, https://doi.org/10.1787/ff7c8ac4-en.

Comité interministériel à l'intégration (2018), *S'investir ensemble*, https://www.interieur.gouv.fr/Actualites/Communiques/Comite-Interministeriel-a-l-Integration.

Diaz Ramirez, M., T. Liebig, C. Thoreau and P. Veneri (2018), "The integration of migrants in OECD regions: A first assessment", *OECD Regional Development working papers*, No. 2018/01, OECD Publishing, Paris, https://doi.org/10.1787/fb089d9a-en.

DIHAL (2017), *Rapport d'activité 2015-2016 : Construire et innover ensemble pour les personnes sans - abri et mal-logées.*

Epstein, R. (2012), « Politique de la ville, rénovation urbaine, égalité territoriale : quelles est la nature du problème ? », in *Politique de la ville, Perspectives françaises et ouvertures internationales*, Centre d'analyse stratégique- La documentation française, Paris, pp.33-49.

Escalfré-Dublet, A. (2016), *Mainstreaming Immigrant Integration Policy in France*, Migration Policy Institute.

European Commission (2018), *Toolkit on the use of EU funds for the integration of people with a migrant background.*

Eurostat (2017), *Migration and migrant population statistics,* http://ec.europa.eu/eurostat/statistics-explained/pdfscache/17145.pdf.

Giraudon, V. (2009) The multi-level governance of international migration: an unbalanced act?

IAU (2012), *La gouvernance du logement en Île-de-France - Étude relative à la création d'une autorité organisatrice du logement.*

IFOP (2016), *Ifop pour Dimanche Ouest France - Les Français et la crise des migrants en Europe*, Departement Opionion et Stratégies d'Entreprise.

INTI-CITIES, 2009 Benchmarking integration governance in Europe's cities, http://www.integratingcities.eu/integrating-cities/projects/inti-cities.

IPSOS Global Advisor (2016), « Attiude à l'egard de l'immigration et de la crise des réfugiés dans le monde », www.ipsos.fr/sites/default/files/doc_associe/globaldvisor_immigration-et-refugies_fr.pdf.

Karoutchi, R. (2017), « Migrants : les échecs de l'apprentissage du français et des valeurs civiques », *Rapport d'information, No. 660 (2016-2017) fait au nom de la commission des finances du Sénat.*

Kirszbaum, T. (2004), « Discours et pratiques de l'intégration des immigrés. La période des Grands Projets de Ville », *Les annales de la recherche urbaine*, No. 97, pp. 51-59.

Lelévrier, C., C. Rivière, A. Escafre-Dublet and G. Shokry (2017), *Divercities: Dealing with Urban Diversity - The case of Paris,* University of Paris Est-Créteil, Paris.

Mairie de Paris (2017*), Budget primitif*, http://budgetprimitif2017.paris.fr/#/.

Mairie de Paris (2016), *Communication sur l'effort de la collectivité parisienne en faveur de l'intégration des Parisiens immigrés, pour les droits humains, la lutte contre les discriminations et l'égalité femmes-hommes*, Direction de la Démocratie Des Citoyens et des Territoires, Service Égalité, Intégration, Inclusion.

Mairie de Paris (2015a), *Insérer par l'emploi : Plan parisien de l'insertion par l'emploi 2015-2020.*

Mairie de Paris (2015b), *Mobilisation de la communauté de Paris pour l'accueil des réfugiés.*

Ministère de l'Intérieur (2016a), *Circulaire sur les Schémas régionaux d'accueil des demandeurs d'asile*, Paris.

Ministère de l'Intérieur (2016b), *Activité, emploi et chômage des immigrés en 2015, L'essentiel de l'immigration*, Paris.

Noiriel, G. (2002), *Atlas de l'immigration en France*, Autrement, Paris.

OECD (2018a), *Working togetherfor integration of migrants and refugees*, OECD Publishing, Paris, https://doi.org/10.1787/9789264085350-en.

OECD (2018b), *Divided Cities, Understanding intra-urban inequalities*, OECD Publishing, Paris, https://doi.org/10.1787/9789264300385-en.

OECD (2018c), International Migration Outlook, OECD Publishing, Paris, http://dx.doi.org/10.1787/migr_outlook-2018-en.

OECD (2017a), *International Migration Outlook*, OECD Publishing, Paris, https://doi.org/10.1787/migr_outlook-2017-en.

OECD (2017b), *Le recrutement des travailleurs étrangers : France 2017*, OECD publications, Paris, https://doi.org/10.1787/9789264276741-fr.

OECD (2017c), *The Governance of Land Use in France*: *Case studies of Clermont-Ferrand and Nantes Saint-Nazaire*, OECD Publishing, Paris, https://doi.org/10.1787/9789264268791-en.

OECD (2017d), *Multi-level Governance Reforms - Overview of OECD Country Experiences*, OECD Publishing, Paris, https://doi.org/10.1787/9789264272866-en.

OECD (2016a), *International Migration Outlook*, OECD Publishing, Paris, http://dx.doi.org/10.1787/migr_outlook-2016-en.

OECD (2016b), *How is life in France?,* OECD Publishing, Paris, https://doi.org/10.1787/how_life-2017-19-en.

OECD (2016c), *Making Cities Work for All - Data and Actions for Inclusive Growth*, OECD Publishing, Paris, https://doi.org/10.1787/9789264263260-en.

OECD (2014) International Migration Outlook, OECD publications, Paris, https://doi.org/10.1787/migr_outlook-2014-en.

OECD (2007), *Linking Regions and Central Governments: Contracts for Regional Development – France*, OECD Publishing, Paris, https://doi.org/10.1787/9789264008755-en.

OECD (2006), *OECD Territorial Reviews: France*, OECD Publishing, Paris, https://doi.org/10.1787/9789264022669-en.

OECD and EU (2015*), Indicators of Immigrant Integration 2015: Settling In*, OECD Publishing, Paris, https://doi.org/10.1787/9789264234024-en.

OFPRA (2017), *Rapport d'activité de l'Office français pour la protection des réfugiés et des apatrides 2016.*

Paris Region (2018), *Paris region – key figures 2018*, https://investparisregion.eu/sites/default/files/key_figures_2018-5_bd_1.pdf.

PETP; Projet Educatif Teritorial de Paris (2015), *Projet éducatif territorial de Paris 2016-2019.*

Pew Research Centre (2016), "Europeans fear wave of refugees will mean more terrorism, fewer jobs", www.pewglobal.org/2016/07/11/europeans-not-convinced-growing-diversity-is-a-good-thing-divided-on-what-determines-national-identity/.

Proietti, P. and P. Veneri (2017), "The location of hosted asylum seekers across regions and cities", paper presented at the 31st OECD Working Party on Territorial Indicators, May 2017.

Safi, M. (2014), « Une refondation manquée : Les politiques d'immigration et d'intégration en France », *La vie des idées*.

Safi, M. (2009), « La dimension spatiale de l'intégration : évolution de la ségrégation des populations immigrées en France entre 1968 et 1999 », *Revue française de Sociologie.*

Salvi del Pero, A. et al. (2016), "Policies to promote access to good-quality affordable housing in OECD countries", *OECD Social, Employment and Migration Working Papers*, No. 176, OECD Publishing, Paris, https://doi.org/10.1787/5jm3p5gl4djd-en.

Schnapper, D. (2008), « Intégration nationale et intégration des migrants : un enjeu européen », *Questions d'Europe*, No. 90, Fondation Robert Schuman.

Schnapper, D. (2007) Qu'est-ce que l'intégration ? Folio Actuel.

Scholten, P. (2014), *TheMulti-level Governance of Migrant Integration - Migration: A COMPAS Anthology*, COMPAS, Oxford.

Scholten, P. and R. Penninx (2016), "The Multi-level Governance of Migration and Integration", in *Integration processes and policies in Europe*, imiscoe research series.

Simon, P. and V. Tiberj (2012), « Les registres de l'identité. Les immigrés et leurs descendants », *Documents de travail*, No. 176, Ined, Paris.

Tache, A. (2018), « Pour une politique ambitieuse d'intégration des étrangers arrivant en France », *Rapport Parlementaire au Premier Ministre en mission auprès du ministre de l'Intérieur.*

UCL INEQ-CITIES Atlas (2017), https://www.ucl.ac.uk/ineqcities/atlas/cities/paris.

UNSD (2017), *International Migration Statistics* (database), https://unstats.un.org/unsd/demographic/sconcerns/migration/migrmethods.htm#B.

Vandendriessche, X. (2012), *Le droit des étrangers*, Dalloz.

Verpeaux, M. (2015), *Les collectivités territoriales*, Dalloz.

Yaouancq, F. and M. Duée (2014), *Dossier : Les sans-domicile en 2012 : Une grande diversité des situations*, INSEE, Paris.

Further Reading

Kleine-Rueschkamp, L. and P. Veneri (forthcoming), "Assessing the Integration of Migrants in OECD regions", OECD Publishing, Paris.

Massey, D. S (1985) Ethnic Residential Segregation: a Theoretical Synthesis and Empirical Review, Sociology and Social Research 69, pp. 315-350.

Preteceille , E. (2006) La segregation sociale a-t-elle augmenté ? Sociétés contemporaines, 62 o 69-93

Tabard, N (1993) Des quartiers pauvres aux banlieues aisées : une représentation sociale du territoire, Economie et statistiques, 10 270, pp 5-22.

Annex A. Allocation of competences in France relevant for migrant integration

The process of decentralisation has been developed through three key steps in France starting in the early 1980s. In 1982, Act 1 of decentralisation begun through the Gaston Deffer law that transferred executive power from the state-designated administrator at the local level to regional and department councils, and financially compensated such transfers through local taxes and a decentralisation grant (OECD, 2006; OECD, 2007; OECD, 2017c). In 2003-2004, Act 2 of decentralisation strengthened regions and recognised them in the Constitution as local autonomous bodies with financial autonomy (the compensation principle was introduced in the constitution) and transferred to regions new competences (i.e. vocational training) (OECD, 2006; OECD, 2007; OECD, 2017c). Through the MAPTAM law in 2014, Act 3 of decentralisation, responsibilities of each government level were clarified and the competences of métropoles (which only apply to large urban areas) strengthened. The 2015 NOTRE law transferred competences to regions and inter-municipalities at the expense of departments (Verpeaux, 2015).

Allocation of competences in France relevant for migrant integration

National level
Ministry of Interior: The DGEF oversees migration matters, defines national policy Prefectures: first registration and deliverance of identity cards for foreign residents, oversee asylum seekers' accommodation system which is managed by partner associations, oversee asylum procedure OFII: In charge of recently arrived regular foreign population; CIR contract and language learning courses, manage, reception of asylum seekers (manages the DNA, redirect asylum seekers to temporary accommodation, allocates the ADA) OFPRA: administers right to asylum in France
Ministry of Territorial Cohesion. Defines national policies in urban planning and housing CGET: City policy DIHAL: Housing for reinstalled and geographically mobile migrants
Ministry of Education: Defines national policy (including Priority Education) and finances school content
Ministry of Employment: Defines national policy on integration of the unemployed into the labour market
Region level: Competences on economic development, secondary education logistics (i.e. infrastructure, building and maintaining high schools), vocational training, transport
Métropole du Grand Paris: Urban Policy
Department: Social policy and welfare allowances (RSA allocation, protection of children) and Education (i.e. infrastructure, building and maintaining first half of secondary schools
Municipality: Education (infrastructure, building and maintaining of kindergartens and primary schools), Housing and urban planning (i.e. apply national regulations for affordable and social housing), Social action and health support (CASVP), language courses through the municipality and support to associations, public space
Non-governmental organisations: Partner with the prefectures for PADA register and management of shelter for asylum seekers; Language courses; social action, food aid and maraudes; legal advice.

Annex B. The Asylum process and legislation in France

Asylum legislative framework

In France asylum law establishes two sorts of international protection status: refugee and subsidiary protection. There are other specific mechanisms to access the refugee status i.e. (1) relocation schemes within the collective responsibility of EU member states; (2) resettlement; (3) asylum visas for specific vulnerable categories.

Recent years have been marked by changes in asylum legislation. In July 2014, the government presented two draft laws on immigration and asylum. The asylum law passed on July 2015 and came into force in November 2015 granting new rights to asylum seekers (i.e. automatically suspends decisions after appeals have been heard by the National Court of Asylum (CNDA), including fast-tracked cases; allows asylum seekers to take advice from the French Refugee Protection Agency (OFPRA), in line with EU directives; provides for improved assessment of and allowance for vulnerabilities at all stages of the application process (for those in poor health, female victims of violence, minors, etc.) (OECD, 2016a).

Another essential aspect of the law is that it has sped up the processes of application as the target was to be able to process asylum application in an average of nine months by the end of 2016. In 2016, according to numbers provided by the Ministry of Interior, the procedure lasted around 14 months. To prevent large numbers of asylum seekers from being concentrated in given parts of the country and to offer quality accommodation and social services, the new law has also set up a compulsory accommodation system (OECD, 2016a).

In February 2018 the national government produced a new asylum bill (*Loi Colomb*) engaged in reducing to six months the length of instruction of asylum claims (appeal included), which would especially apply to Île-de-France where the concentration of asylum seekers makes the procedure longer. It aims at reducing the time in the phases of registration (the asylum application would be processed under the accelerated procedure after 90 days of time once entered in the national territory, instead of 120 days previously), instruction and judgment. The law proposal has also reduced the time available for appealing the rejection of the protection status (from a month to 15 days).[1] This law is under discussion at the moment of drafting this case and so its final characteristics cannot be presented here.

The asylum process step by step

1. PADA: Since 2015, all asylum seekers need to address the Reception Platform for Asylum Seekers (PADA, *Plateforme d'accueil pour les demandeurs d'Asile*) where a partner NGO informs them about asylum, requests online the first interview for asylum seekers registered at the single desk GUDA (see below (2)) and assists them through administrative procedures. In Paris, the CAFDA PADA

is in charge of receiving families and the France Terre d'Asile PADA handles single adults. Long delays for reception and saturation in the Parisian PADAs were indicated through OECD meetings.

2. GUDA: Since 2015, asylum seekers need to present themselves to the single desk ("*Guichet unique*" GUDA) which unites the services of the prefecture and the OFII to register as asylum seekers. The prefecture registers their identity and information and determine the European country eligible for their asylum request. If entitled to request asylum in France, the OFII inscribes the asylum seeker in the National Mechanism of Reception (*Dispostif national d'accueil* DNA) and evaluates the individual situation and its vulnerability, opening its right to the economic allowance for asylum seekers (ADA) and formulates if possible an accommodation proposal. If not considered as an asylum seeker, the person is required to leave the country or enters in a phase of irregularity.
3. OFPRA interview: Once registered, the asylum seeker can introduce his or her request to the OFPRA which independently examines the request. At the OFPRA, a personal interview is organised between the asylum seeker and a "Protection Officer" in which the former present the details of the claim through an interpreter. Since the 2015 Asylum Law, asylum seekers and refugees can be accompanied by a lawyer or a representative of an accredited association in the interview.
4. OFPRA decision: After the personal interview, OFPRA decides about the asylum request and notifies the asylum seeker. The average length of the process is 14 months and the 2018 reform of the asylum law aims at reducing it to 6 months. If the request is approved, the asylum seeker becomes a refugee or a beneficiary of subsidiary protection. If the OFPRA rejects the application, the asylum seeker can appeal and contest the decision in the National Court of Asylum Law (*Cour nationale du droit d'asile*, CNDA) which can approve the petition for international protection or reject it. In the former case, the asylum seeker becomes a "*debouté*" and needs to leave the country just like all irregular migrants. The 2018 Asylum reform reduces the delay of appeal to the CNDA from 1 month to 15 days after the rejection at the OFPRA.
5. Once asylum seekers become status-holders, they enter the "*Droit commun*" and are not entitled anymore to government-provided temporary accommodation dedicated to asylum seekers (*hébergement*). Theoretically, recognised refugees should be able to access autonomously either the private or social housing system.

The accommodation system for asylum seekers in France

The accommodation system for asylum seekers in France is complex and composed of multiple forms of facilities according to the administrative status of the beneficiary.[2] There are three main types of temporary accommodation for asylum seekers connected to the National Reception System (*Dispositif national d'accueil, DNA*) in which the OFII can find available spaces for vulnerable asylum seekers: CADA, HUDA and AT-SA.

1. CADA (*Centre d'accueil pour demandeurs d'asile*) are the main type of reception facilities (40 450 spots across France in January 2018) offering housing as well as extensive administrative and social support provided by social workers. Three key actors participate in the governance of CADA: the Asylum Direction (within the Directorate for Foreigners under the Interior Ministry, DGEF), the Prefects and NGOs managing the centres. The asylum direction coordinates and finances these

structures through a call for projects that is disseminated by the Prefect which allocates their management to an association (i.e. COALIA, France Terre d'Asile, etc.).

2. HUDA (*Hébergement d'urgence pour demandeurs d'asile)* are emergency facilities intended to compensate for the lack of beds in regular reception centres. Theoretically, their mission is to accompany asylum seekers before their entry into CADA. These structures are managed directly at local level, and the services they can provide vary strongly from one centre to another. For instance, this category includes hotel stays, with no administrative and social assistance, as well as more stable structures, in which the housing and social support's quality can be compared to the services offered in CADA. All asylum applicants, including people under the Dublin status, can access these facilities. They are also managed by partner associations (e.g. Adoma, Coalia etc.) and there are 21 000 HUDA spots in France.
3. The AT-SA (*Accueil temporaire – Service de l'asile)* is an emergency reception facility managed at national level that is mainly used to provide housing for asylum seekers settled in overcrowded territories, such as the Paris area, or in order to be able to dismantle makeshift camps. These structures (5 776 spots at the national level) have also been involved in the accommodation of asylum applicants in the context of the European relocation scheme.

Further, since 2015, along with the traditional structures of reception and accommodation of asylum seekers (CADA, AT-SA and HUDA), new specialised shelter categories were created in a context of camp dismantling. They aim to be transit shelters covering the period between camps or homelessness and accessing the *Dispositif national d'accueil* for asylum seekers. The CAO (Centres of Reception and Orientation) were created by the national government in 2015 when the Calais camp was dismantled. The CAOs are spread across the national territory except in Île-de-France to relieve the Parisian overcrowding. There are temporary centres (between 3 and 6 months) for shelter and administrative and health support. In the Parisian region, the CHUM (*Centre d'hébèrgement d'urgence pour Migrants*) are equivalent to CAO and temporarily host people after makeshift camps have been dismantled in Paris. CHUM are financed by the Prefecture (DRHIL) under BOP 177 and managed by partner NGOs.

Formally outside the asylum system but playing a critical role in hosting asylum seekers and refugees are the CHUs (*Centres d'hebergement d'urgence*, i.e. Emergency Accommodation Centres). These are universal structures managed by the SAMU Social providing shelter for homeless people in Paris which, since 2015, received many asylum seekers, especially after camp evacuation.

Annex C. List of participants in this case study

Central government and delegations

- Raphaël Sodini, Ministère de l'Intérieur, DGEF, Directeur de l'asile
- Célia Caumont, Ministère de l'Intérieur, DGEF, Direction de l'asile, Chef de la division Intégration de l'intégration des réfugiés
- Agnès Fontana, Ministère de l'intérieur, DGEF, Directrice de l'accueil, de l'accompagnement des étrangers et de la nationalité
- Mourad Derbak, Office français pour la protection des réfugiés et des apatrides, Directeur de la Division Europe
- Patrick Veillescazes, Chef de cabinet, Préfecture de la région Île-de-France
- Silvain Mathieu and Faustine Masson, DIHAL

Municipal Level

- Dominique Versini, Adjointe à la maire de Paris en charge des Solidarités, lutte contre l'exclusion, accueil des réfugiés et protection de l'enfance
- Colombe Brossel, Adjointe à la maire Sécurité, prévention, quartiers populaires et intégration
- Anne-Charlotte Leluc, Conseillère Solidarités, Cabinet de Dominique Versini, Adjointe à la maire de Paris en charge des Solidarités, lutte contre l'exclusion, accueil des réfugiés et protection de l'enfance
- Charlotte Schneider, Chef de projet Réfugiés et migrants, Cabinet de Dominique Versini, Adjointe à la maire de Paris en charge des Solidarités, lutte contre l'exclusion, accueil des réfugiés et protection de l'enfance
- Vanessa Benoit, Centre d'Action Sociale de la Ville de Paris (CASVP)
- Chloé Mons, Cheffe de projet grande cause lutte contre l'exclusion, Secrétariat Général de la Ville de Paris
- Sophie Rosso, Cabinet de M. Missaka, Adjoint à la maire de Paris, Urbanisme, Architecture, Développement économique et attractivité
- Magali Robert, Cabinet de de M. Veron, Adjointe à la maire de Paris, Démocratie Locale, Participation citoyenne, vie associative, jeunesse, emploi
- Thomas, Fansten, Cabinet de M. Klugman, Adjoint en charge des relations internationales et de la francophonie

Civil society organisations and International Organizations

- Camila Rios, Kiron
- Julia Tran Thanh, Kiron
- Camille Soulier, Kiron
- Sabreen Al Rassace, Permanence Réfugiés Syriens Revivre

- Aurelie El Hassak Marzorate, Emmaus
- Heloise, Nio, Ecole Thot
- Geneviève Domenach-Chich, La cimade
- Davis Robert, Singa
- Inesse Benmohamme, Singa
- Perrine Jospin, Armée du salut
- Blandine Lebrun, Tandem réfugiés
- Blanche Pichot de Champleury Langues Plurielles
- Helena Velediaz, Langues Plurielles
- Pierre Frotté, Solidarité Jean Merlin
- Violette Debarbouille, Action Emploi Réfugié
- Stéphanie Rapin, UNHCR Paris
- Rolince Mbungo, UNHCR Paris
- Céline Schmitt, UNHCR Paris
- Florence Boreil, UNHCR Paris

ORGANISATION FOR ECONOMIC CO-OPERATION AND DEVELOPMENT

The OECD is a unique forum where governments work together to address the economic, social and environmental challenges of globalisation. The OECD is also at the forefront of efforts to understand and to help governments respond to new developments and concerns, such as corporate governance, the information economy and the challenges of an ageing population. The Organisation provides a setting where governments can compare policy experiences, seek answers to common problems, identify good practice and work to co-ordinate domestic and international policies.

The OECD member countries are: Australia, Austria, Belgium, Canada, Chile, the Czech Republic, Denmark, Estonia, Finland, France, Germany, Greece, Hungary, Iceland, Ireland, Israel, Italy, Japan, Korea, Latvia, Lithuania, Luxembourg, Mexico, the Netherlands, New Zealand, Norway, Poland, Portugal, the Slovak Republic, Slovenia, Spain, Sweden, Switzerland, Turkey, the United Kingdom and the United States. The European Union takes part in the work of the OECD.

OECD Publishing disseminates widely the results of the Organisation's statistics gathering and research on economic, social and environmental issues, as well as the conventions, guidelines and standards agreed by its members.

OECD PUBLISHING, 2, rue André-Pascal, 75775 PARIS CEDEX 16
(85 2018 21 1 P) ISBN 978-92-64-30585-4 – 2018

www.ingramcontent.com/pod-product-compliance
Lightning Source LLC
LaVergne TN
LVHW081415110826
845149LV00010B/1755

9789264305854